G000244565

This book makes compe
with care and clarity in it
about love, sex and ma
joyful thing that is – to s
that the Bible describes. C
within the boundaries He prescribes brings with it a mind-
stretching and heart-warming reminder of God our Saviour's
love for His bride the church. No couple will read this without
benefit, and every Christian should rejoice in how much
deeper, richer, more joyful and long lasting the Bible's view
on the matter is than that offered by the world! A brilliant
little book and a healthy corrective!

Wallace & Lindsay Benn
Retired from Church of England ministry

Adrian and Celia take us back to God's Word and explore
how sex is described in the Bible. By doing so they open our
eyes to profound truths; as husband and wife experience the
close oneness of sexual intimacy they not only point towards
a greater truth (Christ and the church) but they also learn and
discover something of the very nature of God Himself. They
draw out practical implications from this for married couples,
whilst also providing helpful pastoral direction for those for
whom this is an area of disappointment and difficulty. There
is also a superb annotated list of further helpful reading. This
excellent short book will enrich any marriage.

Greg & Harriet Strain
Spicer Street Church, St Albans

When it comes to thinking about God's good gift of sexual
intimacy we can choose to drink from the springs of living
water or from the cracked cisterns of the world. This book is
a helpful and honest way of drinking from the former. A great
introduction for those who don't know what God has to say
about His good gift. And a profitable reminder for those who
have already searched the Scriptures.

Robin & Ursula Weekes
Emmanuel Church, Wimbledon

AND THEN HE KNEW HER ...

A biblical view of sex

ADRIAN & CELIA REYNOLDS

CHRISTIAN
FOCUS

Adrian Reynolds is Director of Ministry of the Proclamation Trust and also serves as associate minister at East London Tabernacle Baptist Church.

Copyright © Adrian & Celia Reynolds 2015

paperback ISBN 978-1-78191-584-4
epub ISBN 978-1-78191-621-6
mobi ISBN 978-1-78191-620-9

Published in 2015
by
Christian Focus Publications, Ltd.
Geanies House, Fearn, Ross-shire,
IV20 1TW, Scotland, United Kingdom.
www.christianfocus.com

Cover design by Daniel van Straaten

Printed by
Bell and Bain, Glasgow

CONTENTS

Introduction 7

1 The way of the world 11

2 The language of love 27

3 The big picture 49

4 So much more 71

5 What if...? 95

6 A closing word 107

Further Reading 110

With grateful thanks to God for our marriage

(1991 – present)

INTRODUCTION

Do we really need a book about sex?
    After all, it's a subject that's as old as humanity. Can there really be anything more to say? Can Christians really contribute anything that hasn't already been said by the world? Our weekend newspaper contains a sexual advice column. It doesn't set out to be Christian; however the advice offered is often wise and useful for couples and would not be out of place in a Christian counselling session.[1] What more have Christians to add? There are already far too many Christian *marriage* books. In fact, it seems you can't be a high profile couple

---

1. Suzi Godson writing in *The Times* newspaper *Weekend* supplement (London edition). We have a different worldview from Suzi, of course, but her advice for married couples is often astoundingly good.

in ministry unless you've penned one. There are also lots of Christian books about sex, though (it must be said) they vary enormously in usefulness.

However, Christians struggle with more fundamental issues. What is sex for? Why is it important? Why does it belong only in marriage? Answering these basic questions will give all Christians (married, singles, those engaged, teenagers) a more robust biblical theology of sex which will help us both face the world and ensure sex is put in its proper context in the Christian life.

This is a real battleground for believers today. As we write, one well-known newspaper journalist is once again calling for a rethink on sexual values:

> The time has come to recalibrate the expression 'sex scandal' because if the Brooks-Newmark story [the current scandal] teaches us anything, it is how old and silly and out of touch it makes half of society look .... The internet has left the old morality way behind and frankly, in order to be credible, we need to find new rules of engagement.[2]

This is the world in which we live: a world in which animal welfare (to quote the article) is more important and of a significantly higher moral value than what we do in the privacy of our bedrooms. And Christians are not just out of step. We are on the back foot; defensive, apologetic even. It's as though the Bible has *nothing* positive to say about this important subject.

---

2.   Melanie Reid writing in *The Times* newspaper (London edition), *We're far too prim for this age of cybersex*, 30 September 2014.

Our aim, therefore, is simple. It's to introduce the subject biblically, briefly and directly. This short book – which won't take you long to read – does not aim to answer every question. But we trust and pray that by taking on board the simple truths we try to convey, you will have a good grounding to see what the Bible teaches, applying these realities to your own life and making sure that your view of sex is no more *and* no less than God intends.

Most of this material started life as part of a marriage enrichment programme that we've run for many years It's been focused and reworked over that time and we're grateful for those who have helped us shape it. We've also been influenced by what we've read about marriage and sex – particular mention should go to our work colleague, Christopher Ash, and regular conference colleague, John Piper. Their marriage books are first class[3] and a short volume such as this can only hope to be a brief summary of others' more robust work.

As always, we bear responsibility for what we've written; however, a number of friends have provided useful input. We're particularly grateful for the theological and pastoral insights of two wise colleagues, Dr Jonathan Griffiths and Dr Tim Ward. This short book is the stronger for their assistance. We are also thankful to John van Eyk, minister

---

3. Of Christopher Ash's two excellent books, the longer, more technical volume is the best: *Marriage: Sex in the service of God* (Nottingham: Inter-Varsity Press, 2003). John Piper's *This Momentary Marriage* (Nottingham: Inter-Varsity Press, 2009) is a great primer both for those getting married and those already married. It includes a clear and helpful chapter on singleness.

of the Tain/Fearn congregation of the Associated Presbyterian Church for his insightful help.

We also ought to say that a book about the Bible's view of sex is going to be forthright because the Bible is forthright. We hope that this book might be read by all Christians, but we want to warn you that if you are of a more sensitive disposition, there may be parts which – whilst biblical – are a little challenging because of the situation you are in right now.

For most, however, we trust the Bible's teaching will encourage you and – whether you are single or married – help you appropriately treasure this gift from God.

Adrian & Celia Reynolds
London 2015

1

THE WAY OF THE WORLD

Is the world obsessed with sex?
Raquel Welch, a sex symbol in the 1960s and 70s, has said that we have equated happiness in life with as many orgasms as you can possibly pack in. Do you agree?

Poll in the Guardian Newspaper, 13 March 2012

Response: Yes – 73 per cent.

Sex is all around us. It always has been, of course. How else can we explain our presence in this world? Here's a clue: the stork did not bring us. But even the most sceptical observer would have to admit that sex is now front and centre when, even a generation ago, things would have been much more reserved. Take cinema. Films with an 18 certificate can now be shown in mainstream cinemas even when they include explicit real (not simulated) sexual scenes. Such graphic depiction was unthinkable even twenty years ago. We see similar patterns in other media. In school, sex education is more graphic and direct. Much to our children's amusement and amazement, it really is true that thirty years ago sex and reproduction lessons at our local grammar schools focused just on the rabbits.

Let's be honest: the ability to talk candidly about sex is not necessarily a bad thing. We must recognise that along with more liberal attitudes towards some forms of sex, there are also increasing taboos. Behaviour that was tolerated in the 1970s, for example, is now properly considered inappropriate. Some 1970s 'family' viewing is rightly considered sexist and demeaning today.[1] Sexual abuse is more widely recognised and far more frequently reported. All that is good.

Nevertheless, it is impossible to live in the Western world and not be bombarded by the world's view of sex. It's everywhere. As the Hollywood actress Sharon Stone admits, 'It's not just Hollywood. Everyone is obsessed with sex.'[2] Christians can react in one of two ways. We could retreat behind the barricades and try to make sure that the subject of sex is one which never passes our lips. As we hope to show you, this kind of head-in-the-sand approach does not do justice to the Bible's view.

---

1. For example, U.K. sketch shows such as *The Two Ronnies* starring Ronnie Corbett and Ronnie Barker and the entire *Carry On* genre.

2. Writing in, of all places, *The Hindustan Times* (Delhi edition), 13 May 2014.

Alternatively, we could embrace the candidness of the world and ensure we keep up. We think we need sermons on sex, small groups discussing sex, help-lines, books, counsellors and so on. Some measure of that is possibly helpful, but there is a great danger of making sex *too* important. It's perfectly possible for Christians to idolise sex as much as the world. In this book, we're going to try to put forward a third way, what we think is a robust and healthy biblical view. But first, if we're going to embrace such a view, we need to understand what we're up against.

Why?

It's simple. One of the key challenges that Christians face is that of worldliness. Our calling as followers of Jesus is to reject this pressure and take the narrow way of the Master.

> Do not conform to the pattern of this world, but be transformed by the renewing of your mind. Then you will be able to test and approve what God's will is – his good, pleasing and perfect will (Rom. 12:2).

Worldliness may be to think too little of sex (though that seems increasingly unusual in today's climate) or too much. Either way, we need to reject *conform*ity and embrace *transform*ity. Step 1 of that process is understanding the pressures the world places on us when it comes to sex. We need to spot when we are being conformed. So, let us suggest at least five ways the world thinks about sex.

SEX AS A COMMODITY

For many people today, sex is nothing more than a commodity to be traded. It's a cash alternative to be used to bargain, negotiate and blackmail, albeit (it must be said) a particularly enjoyable one. Anecdotally, we heard about one Christian University campus GP complaining that almost 80 per cent of the cases he sees are to do with sexually transmitted diseases.[3] University students are trading sex, he said, as keen young boys might trade football stickers.

That admittedly anecdotal evidence is borne out in the largest sexual attitudes survey that is regularly carried out in the U.K. It has been running since 1991 – not even twenty-five years. In that short period, the average number of sexual partners for women aged 16-44 has risen from 3.7 to 7.7 with no sign of a let up in the increase. Although only 1 per cent of 16-44 year olds had chlamydia (a sexually transmitted disease) this proportion rose by a startling 500 per cent for women aged 18-19.[4] Significantly, respondents to the survey were asked whether one night stands were acceptable. Approximately 10 per cent of those in the 65-74 age group agreed that they were, but this figure rose to 20 per cent in males up to the age of thirty-four.

If the statistics alarm us, they are right to do so. In broad terms, people are much more casual

---

3. This information came in a private conversation, but we've no reason to doubt the accuracy of the data.

4. The National Survey of Sexual Attitudes and Lifestyle is available for free online at www.natsal.ac.uk and also reported in U.K. Medical Journal *The Lancet*.

about sex. It has been detached from relationship (something we shall see the Bible condemns) and has become a tradable commodity. For example, a national British newspaper recently reported the case of a woman who had sex with twenty-three men in return for a free holiday.[5]

It's true that research has largely discredited the 'sex as commodity' theory where one partner (typically a woman) only allows another to have sex if he, for example, fulfils certain jobs around the house.[6] Nevertheless, the increase of casual sex and detachment from relationship (reflected in the increased acceptance of one night stands and average number of sexual partners) demonstrates an attitude towards sex that sees it as something that can be cheaply offered or easily accepted.

Chastity (abstinence from sex) is no longer a virtue, but something to mock or laugh at. The 2005 Hollywood blockbuster *The Forty Year Old Virgin* starring Judd Apatow and Steve Carrell did just that. The opening sentence of the studio blurb encourages us to express amazement at the social freak who is the main star: 'Andy at the age of forty *still* hasn't had sex' (italics added).[7]

In 2011, U.K. Member of Parliament Nadine Dorries introduced a members' bill to include abstinence teaching as part of the sex education

---

5. *Drugged up reveller bites people in Magaluf, Daily Star* Newspaper (London edition), 4 July 2014.

6. See, for example, the article in *The Independent* Newspaper, *20 times more sex?* by Ally Fogg, 1 February 2014.

7. See www.imdb.com/title/tt0405422 accessed July 2014.

given to girls at state schools. 'We need to let young girls know that to say no to sex when you are under pressure is a cool thing to do,' she said. MP Chris Bryant scorned the idea. 'This is the daftest piece of legislation I have ever seen.'[8] Such mockery is commonplace in schools and workplaces, not just the House of Commons.

Perhaps, though, the tradable nature of sex is seen most obviously in the proliferation of pornography, especially through the Internet. It would be naïve to suggest that such material has not always been around in whatever media could be used (as a quick trip to see the Greek artefacts in the British Museum will confirm!). Nevertheless, it is also obvious that the access the Internet affords, matched with the privacy it confers, is giving us (and especially men) a view that sex is something which can be bought and sold (or, if possible, obtained for free).

Of course, some might claim that those who participate in producing pornography do so out of free choice. Such an argument may satisfy the consciences of those who view the material, but it is almost certainly untrue and, anyway, it does not – from a Christian point of view – make pornography morally right. And, moreover, the view of sex it portrays does *not* stay in private, even if it begins there. It carries over onto the streets. Literally, in some cases: according to information website www.procon.org prostitution is now only fully prohibited in three Western European countries

---

8. Reported by the BBC News, 4 May 2011.

(Norway, Spain, Sweden), though even in these places sex workers and those who traffic them find ways around laws and regulations. It is a well-researched phenomenon that young people are greatly influenced by both the looks and actions of those who appear in pornographic magazines and movies.

SEX AS A RIGHT

Why is sex traded in this way as something that is 'mine' to give, barter or sell? It is in part because the world sees sexual pleasure as an inalienable right. In 2000, the World Health Organisation adopted the World Association of Sexology's Declaration of Sexual Rights.[9] The declaration contains eleven 'rights' together with a preamble. The statement begins:

> Sexual rights are universal human rights based on the inherent freedom, dignity and equality of all human beings.

Some of the statements contain clauses which Christians would heartily endorse. For example, the rights exclude 'all forms of sexual coercion, exploitation and abuse at any time and situations in life.' However, there is also a 'right' to sexual pleasure:

> Sexual pleasure, including autoeroticism,[10] is a source of physical, psychological, intellectual and spiritual well-being.

---

9.   The full text is available at www.sexology.org

10. A technical way of describing self-pleasure, most commonly masturbation.

Notwithstanding the poor theology (sexual pleasure cannot be a *source* of spiritual well-being as Christians would understand it), this is a remarkable statement. The detailed chapter behind this 'right' (Chapter 8 of the Millennium Declaration) condemns many religious groups for removing any concept of sexual pleasure from the act of sex itself. As we shall see, within the context of marriage, pleasure is an important part of sex. It is an altogether greater step, however, to identify this as a basic human right. Nevertheless, humanity increasingly believes it has the right to personal happiness, and it is perhaps therefore no surprise that the World Health Agency adopted this provision, despite its contentious nature, especially amongst faith groups from the U.S.A.

For singles, such thinking places an increasing emphasis on masturbation, or what is more scientifically described as autoeroticism. Whereas sex education – certainly when we were at school – once focused on the mechanics of sex and sexual reproduction ('how it all works'), the subject is now taught more broadly. Some of that is no doubt welcome – some sex education material stresses the importance of relationship context, something that is also key to a Christian understanding, even though our view of the appropriate context might be different.

However, some of the material taught to our children is solely about self-pleasure. 'Masturbation is encouraged and – shock horror – the clitoris is mentioned' gloats a newspaper report deriding

Christians' objections to one particular school's programme.[11] In a world where sexual pleasure is seen as a right in or out of sexual relationships, this is the natural consequence. It is perhaps no accident that the use of pornography amongst teens is so worryingly high. Indeed, it seems almost hypocritical to – on the one hand – bemoan the high incidence of teen use of pornography, as the world sometimes does, whilst – on the other – assert every human's right to self-pleasure.

SEX AS A PRIVATE MATTER

All of this reflects the privatisation of sex. We don't mean that previously sex was a public act in the sense that others could see it. No, historically it has always been an intimately private act, appropriately conducted out of the gaze of others. Rather, we mean that, increasingly, people believe no one else has the right to dictate what is done in the privacy of our own bedrooms. This was a key argument in the liberalisation of homosexuality seen, for example, in the Wolfenden Report published in 1957. This report argued for:

> ... the importance society and the law ought to give to individual freedom of actions in matters of private morality ... there must remain a realm of private morality and immorality which is, in brief and crude terms, not the law's business.[12]

---

11. This particular report is from *The Guardian* newspaper (London edition) 8 March 2010, commenting on material produced by Sexual Health Sheffield for schools work.

12. Reported in *The Times* newspaper (London edition) 5 September 1957, p.10.

At this stage, the report was still drawing distinctions between behaviour that was morally acceptable or not. Even some actions considered 'immoral' were a private matter, the report argued. Later, that moral distinction was to disappear and most sexual behaviour between consenting adults has now become a matter of personal privacy. Many of the recent objections to the church's position on homosexuality have been the right of others to dictate what might or might not be done in private.

SEX AS AN EVIL

The argument of privacy, however, is remarkably slippery. Just because an act happens in private does not make it morally right, as indeed the law in the U.K. still recognises. In this maelstrom of sexual activity, it comes as something of a surprise to know that sex is still seen by society as an evil if it takes place in certain contexts. As one U.K. Christian leader has written, 'Christians tend to see the past fifty years as a time of increasing moral degeneracy, marked by sexual liberation and promiscuity. However the reality is not quite so simple.'[13] It's true, there have been great changes made in terms of private practice and what is acceptable. Chief amongst these is the legalisation of homosexuality in 1967 and other practices which were previously considered taboo are now considered acceptable in law, if not always socially.

---

13. John Stevens, National Director of the Fellowship of Independent Evangelical Churches, writing at www.john-stevens.com accessed July 2014.

This is not, however, a one-way street. For most of Queen Victoria's reign, the age of consent was 12, raised to 13 in 1875 and 16 in 1885, where it remains, despite pressure to see it lowered. There are now legal prohibitions for those in certain roles: under the U.K. Sexual Offences Act 2003, it is illegal for a school teacher (or someone in a 'position of trust') to have sex with someone aged 16-18 even though both may be considered as consenting adults. Moreover, sexual abuse is much more widely defined and understood to include practices which might in previous generations have been considered 'fooling about!'[14]

So, both legally and socially, we recognise that context is important in defining whether sex is good or bad. The law (at least) recognises that certain relationships cross the boundaries and are unacceptable, if not (in the case of sexual predators) evil. A 22-year-old and a 17-year-old might have a consensual relationship and it may be either legal or illegal depending on their particular role in society.

This confusion does give rise to some anomalies. Recent arguments for a change in the law to allow so-called gay marriage included the argument that those who loved one another should be free to marry. However, the law (and, up to now, society too) recognises that this is not a valid argument. As well as those in positions of trust, close family

---

14. A further example would be the criminalisation of marital rape, a relatively recent addition to the statute book (early 1990s).

members, for example, are not free to marry.[15] Interestingly, in our apparently liberal sexual society, there is still a strong reaction against those who challenge this status quo: an Australian judge, Garry Nielson, is being investigated for comments he made suggesting that incest could soon become socially acceptable.[16]

There is here a point of connection between what Christians believe and what the world believes. As we are going to see, context matters for Christians. What makes sex right or wrong for Christians is the context in which it takes place. We have tended to reduce the morality of sex down to individual acts rather than the setting in which they happen. This places us unnecessarily out of line with the way the world thinks about such matters. If Christians could find ways to speak about context, we would at least be understood by the world – even if we found ourselves disagreeing with the world about where those boundaries were drawn. Perhaps this would enable Christians to be more 'on the front foot' when it comes to such discussions?

CONCLUSION? SEX IS A GOD

Where does this all leave us? It leaves us with the idolisation of sex. Sex has become, in Western soci-

---

15. This is a point that U.K. Government minister Philip Hammond correctly made in a speech at Royal Holloway Student Union. It was pejoratively picked up in the U.K. press with headlines such as 'Minister likens gay marriage to incest', see, for example, *The Times* newspaper (London edition), 29 January 2013.

16. Reported in *The Daily Telegraph* newspaper (London edition), 14 July 2014.

ety at least – a god to be worshipped, followed and adored at all costs. The world will not talk in these terms, of course. Idolatry is a biblical category and – to many people's ears – a prejudicial one, at that. But one glance at the racks of magazines – whether aimed at men or women – will reveal an obsession with sex that is overwhelming. Books, DVDs, on-line forums are solely devoted to improving sexual techniques as better and better sexual performance is pursued. Medicine will help if you want to increase prowess.[17]

'Was it good for you?' has become the mantra of the age. People's aim is to get into bed, and once there to experience intense personal satisfaction almost, it seems, to the exclusion of all else. Women's magazine *Cosmopolitan* lists 'Love and Sex' on its website categories before any other issue (including fashion, beauty and entertainment). This is what people want to know about and pursue.[18]

Christians should not perhaps be surprised at this. Most idols of the age are good gifts given by God, but put in a wrong place. Made in the image of its Creator, humanity often has a deep, subconscious understanding that a particular thing is good and worthy – whether it be family or community or food or work. Sex is the same. But there is something deeply disturbing about the idolatry of sex – perhaps more so than any other issue. We believe

---

17. Medicines like *Viagra* are developed to address serious and real sexual dysfunction. We are not dismissing these. But, like other medications, they are easily abused to provide abnormal sexual 'highs'.

18. See www.cosmopolitan.co.uk

that this is because of what God designed sex to depict. It is therefore high time we finished surveying the world and turned to what God thinks of this big subject.

CHOOSING A BETTER WAY
Sex, as we shall see, is (in its right context) a good gift from the God who made us. It should not, therefore, surprise us that something pleasurable and intrinsically good is appreciated by the world, even though it has been hijacked so comprehensively. Moreover, as attitudes to sex change (which they seem to do with increasing rapidity) Christians must be prepared to defend a biblical view of sex that is increasingly out of step with the way the world thinks and acts.

We are in two particular dangers. The first danger is that, retreating into our own tribal world, we will become overwhelmingly negative about sex in a way that is sub-biblical. Sex is dirty, unmentionable and should certainly not be pleasurable! The stereotypes of our forefathers is that they thought this way about sex. Perhaps many middle-aged Christians live with this kind of emotional baggage.

It seems to us that, though this is a real danger, it is increasingly unlikely that this is the trap into which Christians might fall today. A second, more immediate danger is that we will be swamped by the world, giving into it and letting it shape our thinking. Even within evangelicalism we must accept this is a present temptation.[19] Here, then, is the reason we have written this book. We've said enough about the book of the world. We now need to consider a better source: the book of the Word. For there we find a remarkably robust and positive view of sex.

19. Indeed, Mark and Grace Driscoll's book on marriage, *Real Marriage* (Nashville, Tennessee: Thomas Nelson, 2012) contains a contentious chapter (chapter 10) which gives Christian couples 'permission' to engage in some surprising (to us, anyway) sexual activities. As Denny Burk helpfully writes, there are 'a whole range of pastoral problems that might be provoked by chapter 10 of the Driscolls' book.' Burk, D. *The Meaning of Sex* (Wheaton, Illinois: Crossway Books, 2013), p.121.

2

THE LANGUAGE OF LOVE

Pompey: What's his offence?
Mistress Overdone: Groping for trouts in a peculiar river.

Measure for Measure, Act I, Scene 2,
William Shakespeare

Abimelech king of the Philistines looked out of a window and saw Isaac laughing with Rebekah his wife.

Genesis 26:8 (ESV)

It's not just Will Shakespeare.

There must be more ways of describing sex than any other human activity. Sleep, work, death, war – all these can be described using dozens of phrases which have entered our language over time. But sex? There must be thousands of expressions: ranging from the quaint to the crude. It may surprise you to know that the Bible also describes sexual intimacy in a variety of ways.[1] It's worth pausing and taking a brief survey because some of the words Bible writers use – inspired by the Holy Spirit – are both breathtakingly beautiful and significantly meaningful. They are sometimes clouded from view in our English translations because we use more direct expressions. But it's worth knowing what's behind phrases such as 'Adam made love to his wife Eve' (Gen. 4:1).

If you listened to previous generations you might think that the Bible says nothing about sex. If you listened to the Baby Boomer generation you might think that the Bible says nothing *except* about sex. Both are wrong. In fact, the Bible is sometimes extremely coy about this most intimate of actions, using language that is so subtle it passes most readers by. At other times, the Bible writers are extraordinarily graphic and direct.

Many people are surprised at the sheer variety of words and phrases used to describe this most intimate of acts. However, there is one thing missing – any direct word to describe sexual union.[2] There is, in positive terms at least, simply no Hebrew equivalent to the verb 'to have sex'. The only pos-

---

1. There's even a book devoted to assessing the way the Bible treats the subject. It's been a great help to us and we're indebted to Smith's careful research, but reading it is not for the faint-hearted. Smith, J., *Sex and Violence in the Bible* (Phillipsburg, New Jersey: P&R Books, 2014).

2. 'Reference to sexual organs and activities is almost invariably couched in euphemistic terms. This is due partly to the limitations of the classical Hebrew language: the modern range of scientific vocabulary did not exist. The language limitation in turn reflects the Hebrew wholistic view of humanity: individual organs often refer metaphorically ... to manifestations of the total self.' Davidson, R., *Flame of Yahweh* (Peabody, MS: Hendrickson, 2007), p.8.

sible candidate for a one-word solution is a noun that is related to the verb 'to lie with' (see below) and which our Bibles sometimes translate 'sexual relations'. It only occurs four times[3], however, and each of these times the sense is of something negative – a practice to be avoided, in other words. It is not describing something holy but rather something profane.

For holy language we have to look beyond the immediate words. And just as in the English language, the words the Bible uses to describe sex teach us something themselves. We're going to see that the Bible is concerned not just for the right or wrong of the sexual act itself, but the setting in which it takes place. Yes, even that is reflected in vocabulary.

Perhaps when you were at school, learning the vocabulary of a foreign language was really, really dull. Maybe so. But we want to show you that when it comes to the Bible, words do matter. So, don't skip over this chapter. It will set us up nicely for some of the key Bible teaching on sex later on in the book. However, it's also important to read this chapter (and, indeed the Bible) putting aside the teenage snigger. Just as an immature adolescent delights with his friends in looking up smutty words in the dictionary, it is perfectly possible to survey the Bible's language in a kind of sniggering, saucy postcard kind of manner. That's especially

---

3.   The four references are Leviticus 18:20, 18:23, 20:15 and Numbers 5:20. The issue is confused because other Hebrew words are also translated in the same way in most of our English translations.

true because we're going to discover that the Bible is sometimes very coy about sex – employing very indirect and discrete words and phrases; however, it is also sometimes very graphic and there are parts of the Bible that make even twenty-first century Westerners (bombarded with sexual language and imagery as they are) blush deeply.

FROM THE BEGINNING

It's worth saying from the start that our English translations don't always reflect the original words that were used when the Bible was first written down. The Bible's original language is Hebrew (for the Old Testament) and Greek (for the New), with a little bit of Aramaic thrown in. Translation is a tricky science and we need to look beyond the English words to see some of the Bible's vocabulary when it comes to sex.

For example, the verb 'to know' is used in Genesis 4:1 which we could translate literally as:

And Adam [or the man] knew Eve his wife.

In modern English versions, this is rendered with literal words (as above), more modern terminology ('The man had sexual relations with his wife'), in colloquialism ('Adam slept with Eve') or even in surprisingly reticent language ('Adam and Eve had a son'). We don't need to analyse each of these. It is enough to see the wide variety of ways each version translates one very simple description for sexual union. This chapter is an attempt to get behind the translated words.

Throughout this book, for the sake of convenience, we're simply going to refer to sex as, well ... sex. Any of the phrases listed above might do, as might a host of other words or colloquialisms. But for now, 'sex' will suffice. It's worth saying that it's a particularly neutral word. It does not, for example, capture any sense of relationship. 'Making love' does that much better. Nor does it imply any commitment between a couple. 'Marital relations' does that much better. Nevertheless, plain old 'sex' will do for now.

SEXUAL UNION B.C.

Let's take a closer look at the Old Testament, before the coming of Christ. As you may know, the language of the Old Testament is Hebrew. Let's begin at the beginning – which is not as you might have thought in Genesis 4 and the verse we looked at above, but two chapters earlier. In fact, there is an even earlier implied reference to sex in the command that God gives to Mr & Mrs Adam in the very first chapter of the Bible: 'Be fruitful and increase in number' (Gen. 1:28). However, the first direct reference almost certainly comes in chapter 2:

> That is why a man leaves his father and mother and is united to his wife and they become *one flesh*. Adam and his wife were both naked, and they felt no shame (Gen. 2:24-25, italics added).

This is an important text. It is quoted by Jesus (for example in Matt. 19:5) and Paul (for example in

1 Cor. 6:16) both to reinforce the proper context for sex and to warn against immorality. For now, however, look at the language used. Adam and Eve are *united* to become *one flesh*. The word 'united' is translated as 'cleave' in older translations.[4] This is not the word that describes the sexual union. Nor, contrary to appearances, is the 'one flesh' language.

Whilst 'one flesh' might seem to be language that describes sex, it is actually something more than that. Jesus Himself equates these words with marriage (Matt. 19:1-11), again representing the marriage bond. Nevertheless, the wording is significant for our purposes. For it is in the context of this union that sexual intimacy takes place. It is the most intimate expression of it. 'One flesh' is not sex itself, but neither is it less than sex: it includes it. As one author has written:

> Sex completes the initiation of the marriage covenant, and every sexual act after the initial consummation is an ongoing affirmation of the husband and the wife's unique union.[5]

So, we should not be surprised when Paul quotes the foundational Genesis text to argue against sleeping with a prostitute. In 1 Corinthians 6, Paul is challenging the laissé faire attitude of the Corinthian Christians: they think they can do whatever they like. No, says the Apostle. For example:

---

4. Perhaps helpfully no longer used, as cleave is one of those words that can have opposite meanings, technically called an autantonym. Here it means to join to, but in most modern usage the meaning of 'cleave' is to cut *something in two*.

5. Burk, p.35.

> Do you not know that your bodies are members of
> Christ himself? Shall I then take the members of
> Christ and unite them with a prostitute? Never!
> Do you not know that he who unites himself with
> a prostitute is one with her in body? For it is said,
> 'The two will become one flesh.' But whoever is
> united with the Lord is one with him in spirit
> (1 Cor. 6:15-17).

We will return to this topic, but for now it is
sufficient to see that 'one flesh' language includes
(and appropriately so) the sexual intimacy that a
husband and wife enjoy. Incidentally, here is a Bible
clue that it is the context of sex which makes it a
good or an evil, just as we saw in the world in the
last chapter. Paul doesn't say it explicitly here, but
from what we could read in chapter 7, we know that
when a husband makes himself one flesh with his
wife sexually, it *does not* threaten the unity we enjoy
with Christ. When he does it with a prostitute, it
does. In other words, it is not the act of sex itself
which somehow challenges union with Christ, it is
the context in which sex takes place.

However, there is a second lesson to draw from
this language. It is that in a marriage and in sexual
intimacy, there is something bigger going on. Sex
is not just sex; marriage is not just marriage. We'll
return to this idea soon.

GOING UNDER-COVER

For most of the Old Testament terminology, however, we must turn to euphemism. A euphemism is
a word or phrase that substitutes for a more direct

or graphic word to avoid the frankness of the original. Although increasingly in the West we use direct language for sex (as, indeed, we are doing in this book), we have long used euphemisms too: to sleep with someone is generally understood to be more than simply sharing a bunk bed.

The Bible speaks about sex this way too. We should not, however, make the mistake of thinking that this means sex is unmentionable and somehow dirty. No, the Bible is overwhelmingly positive about sex in its proper context. We've some of us grown up hearing that sex must never be mentioned, yet the Bible is straightforward and honest about sex. But neither is it right to be always reductionist in our language. Indeed, a limited vocabulary which reduces sex down to an act and nothing more – something, for example, that a man does to a woman – neither reflects the Bible's language nor, we suggest, carries the implied meanings that many Bible words portray.

Let's make a start with the verse we've already looked at. The verb 'to know' occurs throughout the Old Testament – in fact, almost one thousand times. It has a very broad range of meanings:

> [the meanings] range from sensory perception to intellectual process to practical skill to careful attention to close relationship to physical intimacy.[6]

Despite the fact that this word has entered into our folklore and law of the land (in the phrase 'carnal

---

6. VanGemeren, W., *New International Dictionary of Old Testament Theology and Exegesis* (Grand Rapids, Michigan: Zondervan, 1997), Vol. 2, p.410.

knowledge') it is still relatively rare in the Bible. Three of its perhaps ten or so occurrences are right here in Genesis 4 (vv. 1, 17 and 25). Nevertheless, despite its apparent obscurity, we begin to see a little light.

Having sex with someone is more than a physical act. There is some emotional connectivity about it. The word 'conveys very well the fully personal level of true sexual union.'[7] In fact, to add the word 'carnal', as our old law-setters did, is to diminish the Bible meaning. It is not just a particular kind of knowledge: head knowledge, heart knowledge, carnal knowledge and so on. No, the sexual act is not so narrow. It is about whole-person connection. To 'know' someone captures that perfectly.

SHARING THE BED

More common is the language of *sleeping with* or *lying with*. This is a common expression in the Bible as well as in Western society (although becoming less so). It is used in the Bible both positively and negatively to describe acts which are both honourable and those which are contrary to God's laws and purposes, although many of its occurrences describe acts which turn out to be less than ideal – for example, some of the shenanigans of the Patriarchs and their children in the book of Genesis.[8] A classic example of its positive use

---

7. Kidner, D., Genesis, Tyndale Old Testament Commentary (Nottingham, U.K.: Inter-Varsity Press, 1967), electronic edition, quoted by Smith, p.44.

8. For example, Genesis 19:31, Genesis 30:3 and Genesis 38:16. Indeed, the majority of instances of this phrase are negative (Logos Research, Electronic Resource).

(and one we will come back to in chapter 4) comes in the story of David and Bathsheba. This is, in part, a sordid story of illicit sex. But a turning point comes in 2 Samuel 12:13 where the prophet Nathan announces calmly:

> The LORD has taken away your sin. You are not going to die.[9]

From then on, David is back in the purposes of God. The relationship with Bathsheba, though begun in the most unpromising and ungodly of circumstances, becomes the means by which God's great promises to David are fulfilled. And the Scriptures describe not just the birth of the new king, but his conception as well.

> Then David comforted his wife Bathsheba, and he went to her and made love to her. She gave birth to a son, and they named him Solomon (2 Sam. 12:24).

The phrase translated by my Bible 'made love' is the combination of the two Hebrew words that, when translated literally, mean 'lie with' or 'sleep with'. Why is this such a good phrase? It may, at one level, describe the manner of sexual union. Most sex, we guess, happens in the horizontal position.

But at another level, it implies all sorts of things. Sleeping with someone suggests more than an act. It suggests that the two couples enjoy some kind of relationship in which the sex takes place. They

---

9.   I'm grateful to Old Testament scholar John Woodhouse for showing me how key this verse is to the whole story.

go to bed together. They sleep together. They wake up together. Like the verb 'to know', we see a hint of a context for the sexual act. Sex is more than an act, though not less so. This language of sleeping with someone is used around thirty times in the Old Testament, making it the most common of metaphors for sex. Our next phrase runs it a close second, appearing in the text on some two dozen occasions.[10]

ON THE MOVE

The Bible writers often describe sex as 'going to/ into'. A classic example of the use of the phrase occurs in the story of Jacob and Laban. Jacob is overwhelmed with the beauty of cousin Rachel and her 'lovely figure' (Gen. 29:17) and agrees to work for seven years for her hand in marriage. At the end of the tenure, Jacob comes to collect on the deal:

> Then Jacob said to Laban, 'Give me my wife. My time is completed, and I want to make love to her' (Gen. 29:21).

The phrase 'make love' obscures the original which literally reads 'because my days are full, let me go into/to her.'[11] You'll find similar references in Genesis 16:4, 2 Samuel 3:7, Proverbs 6:29 and Ezekiel 23:44. At first, it might seem to be a reference to the coital act itself. After all, in Bible usage it is always the man who 'goes into' the

---

10. These figures are from Smith, p.44.
11. Van Der Merwe, C., *Lexham Hebrew-English Interlinear Bible* (Logos Research, Electronic Resource).

woman. In purely physical terms, this would seem to be an appropriate description.

However, the David and Bathsheba story makes Hebrew experts doubtful about that meaning. In our verse from 2 Samuel quoted above, the author uses this phrase 'go into' before he uses the phrase 'sleep with'. It seems slightly strange for him to repetitively say 'David had sex with Bathsheba, had sex with Bathsheba' unless the first phrase has a deeper meaning. Let commentator Joseph Smith explain it:

> This is not a literal reference to coital penetration; rather, it refers to approaching a woman for the purpose of sexual intercourse, perhaps actually 'going in' to her tent or house.[12]

If Smith is right – and the double usage in 2 Samuel at least suggests he may be – then here again is an inference that sex is more than a mere act of copulation. Entering into someone's abode is a significant matter. It implies trust and relationship as one opens one's dwelling to another. Once again, we have a hint that proper and holy sex should take place within a proper context.

STRIPPED DOWN

There is one more reasonably common phrase which we must consider. It is the phrase which might literally be translated 'to uncover nakedness'. It is used almost entirely negatively, describing illicit sexual liaisons. One example passage will suffice,

---

12.   Smith, p.44.

the so-called Table of Affinity in Leviticus 18:6-19 which details the limits of acceptable sexual practice. The phrase 'uncover the nakedness of' occurs seventeen times.

GETTING MORE OBSCURE

We have not even begun to explore some of the more obscure language the Bible writers employ. When King David tells Uriah the Hittite to 'Go down to your house and wash your feet' (2 Sam. 11:8), he's not calling him to go and have a quick power shower.

> How could I go to my house to eat and drink and make love to [literally, *lie with*] my wife? (2 Sam. 11:11).

Uriah understood exactly what David was saying. David's daughter-in-law uses more poetic language in Song of Songs. This is pretty much as euphemistic as it gets.

> My beloved thrust his hand through the latch-opening (Songs 5:4).

Bible scholars regularly debate the precise meaning of Song of Songs. It's a subject to which we will return. For now, let's read it as it seems to be: a series of love poems between a man and a woman, probably betrothed and leading up to their wedding night. Perhaps a simple reading might take Mrs Solomon describing her hubby coming in the back gate. But such a reading would be out of context with the entirety of the poem, dripping as it is with sexual language and inference. No, it is much more likely to be the most intimate of descriptions.

> What is at one level a dream about the opening of a door is in fact at another level a dream about consummation of the lovers' physical relationship.[13]

Elsewhere, cruder language is often reserved for illicit and sinful liaisons.

> At every street corner you built your lofty shrines and degraded your beauty, spreading your legs with increasing promiscuity to anyone who passed by (Ezek. 16:25).[14]

Here the Lord God is challenging Israel about her spiritual adultery and in a moving, but graphic passage, He describes how He nurtured her from infancy even washing 'the blood from you' (commentators assume this to be virginal blood). In other words, Israel was the Lord's virginal bride, but now she is simply prostituting herself with anyone and everyone.

And, uniquely in Leviticus 18:20, we find the phrase obscured by virtually every English translation, but which literally means 'Don't give your penis to your neighbour's wife.'[15] This is

---

13. Provan, I., *NIV Application Commentary on Ecclesiastes and Song of Songs* (Grand Rapids, Michigan: Zondervan, 2001), p.334.

14. There is a double obscurity here because the phrase 'spread your legs' is more accurately translated 'spread your feet'. Genitals are sometimes described in this way, Smith, p.20. Curiously the normally literal ESV is more coy than the NIV here, employing the paraphrase 'offering yourself'.

15. Davidson, p. 11.

perhaps the most graphic and least euphemistic of all the Old Testament language.

HAVING A LAUGH

Perhaps our favourite Old Testament phrase, however, is the way that Isaac and Rebekah are described in Genesis 26. Isaac and his wife travel to Philistine territory to avoid famine in the land. There, perhaps influenced by his father Abraham's example, he tells the men that Rebekah is 'my sister'. He is afraid that the men might kill him on account of Rebekah. The game is given away by a glance from upstairs.

> Abimelech king of the Philistines looked out of a window and saw Isaac laughing with Rebekah his wife (Gen. 26:8, ESV).

The king immediately recognises that the two are married. 'Behold, she is your wife.' It's difficult to imagine that Abimelech could see that just from a good joke they were sharing. Indeed, my Bible footnote gives it away, 'The Hebrew may suggest an intimate relationship.' It's the same word used in the story of Potiphar's wife and Joseph. She wants him in bed and Joseph resists. Frustrated, the woman traps and then accuses Joseph to her husband.

> That Hebrew slave you brought us came to me to make sport of me [literally *to laugh at me*] (Gen. 39:17).

Whether used of a proper relationship (as in the case of Isaac and Rebekah) or of a potentially illicit

And Then He Knew Her ...

one (Joseph and Potiphar's wife), we see once again that the act of sex goes beyond a mere physical union. Yes, at its holy best, even laughter is an appropriate way to describe loving union.

MAKING IT NEW

On into the New Testament the language changes somewhat. Generally, it is more straightforward and less varied. It's worth noting that the Bible writers are still plain when it comes to talking about sex; it's not a dirty or naughty subject to them. We can see this best in Paul's discussion in 1 Corinthians 7. In this passage, Paul is answering a question that the Corinthian Christians have put to him. He quotes it in the first verse.

> Now for the matters you wrote about: 'It is good for a man not to have sexual relations with a woman.' But since sexual immorality is occurring, each man should have sexual relations with his own wife, and each woman with her own husband. The husband should fulfil his marital duty to his wife, and likewise the wife to her husband. The wife does not have authority over her own body but yields it to her husband. In the same way, the husband does not have authority over his own body but yields it to his wife. Do not deprive each other except perhaps by mutual consent and for a time, so that you may devote yourselves to prayer. Then come together again so that Satan will not tempt you because of your lack of self-control (1 Cor. 7:1-5).

In this one passage we see some of the variety of expressions used to describe sex in the New Testament. The first is in the Corinthian question that Paul replays in verse 1. Here, in the NIV it is translated as 'have sexual relations', but more literally it simply means 'touch'.[16] Although it forms the primary basis of the Corinthian question, it is actually only used here in this sense. However, despite its unique place in Scripture, it is still a word that carries inference, just like the Old Testament phrases we have already seen. The overwhelming usage of the word in the New Testament is found in the gospel accounts of Jesus' healing, for example Luke 5:13:

> And Jesus reached out his hand and touched the man. 'I am willing,' he said. 'Be clean!'

There is something more than mechanical about the use of the word. It implies a connection between the one doing the touching and the one being touched. If that is so, then the sexual euphemism is an appropriate one. Once again, sex is more than a physical act; it involves, in some way, an emotional connection.

When Paul responds to the Corinthians, he does so using three phrases to describe the actual sexual

---

16. The ESV takes a similar line to the 2011 NIV. The older NIV took a broader approach: 'It is good for a man not to marry'. Given the context which follows (which is addressing sex within marriage), the updated NIV and ESV seem to have got the translation about right. 'The idiom "to touch a woman" occurs nine times in Greek antiquity ... and in every other instance, without ambiguity, it refers to having sexual intercourse.' Fee, G., *The First Epistle to the Corinthians* (Grand Rapids, Michigan: Eerdmans, 1987), p. 275.

act. The first of these occurs in verse 2. 'Each man should have *sexual relations* with his own wife' (italics added). This phrase translates a common verb and expression – more literally, each man should '*have* his own wife'. Lest we worry that this sounds somewhat misogynistic, the reverse phrase is included too: 'and each woman her own husband'. In the Greek translation of the Old Testament (that Paul would have known) this is a common way of describing sex.[17] However, even within the New Testament we see this phrase used. Take the example of John the Baptist: John's deathly downfall is in his confrontation with King Herod that is reported in Mark 6.

> For Herod himself had given orders to have John arrested, and he had him bound and put in prison. He did this because of Herodias, his brother Philip's wife, whom he had married. For John had been saying to Herod, 'It is not lawful for you to *have* your brother's wife' (Mark 6:17-18, italics added).

This word stands out from the rest of the Bible vocabulary by virtue of its directness. Indeed, in modern language, it is a vulgarity to describe sex in this way. It might seem to our sensitive ears to be an inappropriate way to talk about that most intimate and private of acts. But, even here, there is something to learn, for the phrase is used both ways – the husband *has* the wife, and the wife

---

17. For example, Deuteronomy 28:30 or Isaiah 13:16, although in both cases the word is used negatively.

has the husband. This is a world away from the misogynistic rap lyric which degrades, as the singer celebrates 'having' various women. There is – at least in the way Paul uses the word – a mutuality about sex which we will do well to heed. Thus, even described in its most basic way, sex is – once again – more than an act.

Secondly, Paul talks in terms of obligation: 'The husband should fulfil his marital duty to his wife, and likewise the wife to her husband.' As with the previous word, there is a clear mutuality here that defies medieval notions of a husband 'owning' or 'possessing' a wife. When it comes to the bedroom, each owes something to the other (a point Paul will make clear in the very next sentence). The phrase 'marital duty' (ESV – 'conjugal rights') is an expansion of the Greek word meaning debt or obligation. It is not particularly common, but is used by Paul in Romans 13:

> Give to everyone what you owe them: if you owe taxes, pay taxes; if revenue, then revenue; if respect, then respect; if honour, then honour (Rom. 13:7).

The verb 'owe' in the first phrase is closely connected to the noun we saw in 1 Corinthians.[18] It means an obligation, duty or debt. If 'having' is one of the most direct ways of describing sex in the Bible, then surely 'duty' is one of the coldest!

---

18. Though the word is repeated later in the sentence in English translations of Romans 13:7, it is only added in to make sense of the whole. It does not reappear in Greek.

In fact, this is exactly the way we imagine Victorian women thought about sex – a necessary evil which should be begrudgingly offered up because it is part of 'doing your duty'. Is that what Paul really means? Reading on in the passage answers the question.

> The wife does not have authority over her own body, but yields it to her husband. In the same way, the husband does not have authority over his own body but yields it to his wife (v. 4).

The language of 'duty' needs to be read in the light of a marriage relationship being about the good of the other. In this context then, 'duty' is not a tiresome task which is dull and boring, and which must be reluctantly offered. Rather, it reflects the other-person centeredness of the marriage relationship. 'Paul's emphasis, it must be noted, is not on "You owe me," but on "I owe you."'[19]

That brings us to the last phrase Paul uses in this short passage. It is the most euphemistic of the three.

> Then come together again so that Satan will not tempt you because of your lack of self-control (v. 5).

The phrase 'come together'[20] translates four Greek words. Literally, we might translate it 'be the same'. In this form, it only appears here, but it does in-

---

19. Fee, p. 280.
20. Used by most mainstream English translations.

troduce another idea that Paul makes use of: an idea of oneness which takes us back to where we started.[21]

Wrapping it up

What has this very brief survey shown us? For one thing, the Bible writers had as much variety in their description of sex as we enjoy today. There's nothing new there. However, more importantly, we've seen that this most passionate and intimate of actions is more than an action. We might talk in terms of the 'sexual act' or 'having sex', but to do so seems to ignore the depth of the vocabulary of sex that the Bible employs. There truly is a language of love.

Sex means something, in other words. It is not an empty gesture or dispassionate activity. It carries meaning and implies relationship – it's about knowing, being with, sleeping with, sharing a house *and* a bed. That's something we need to explore further. Most importantly of all, it seems that something bigger is in view when the Bible talks about sex. That's right and it's understanding this big picture that will transform our thinking about sex and help us answer many of the questions the world wants to throw at us, when it comes to this highly charged issue.

---

21. There is one other way of speaking about sex in the New Testament which we have not included here as it is perhaps rather indirect. It is found in Hebrews 13 and it is the injunction to 'keep the marriage bed pure'. Literally this reads, 'let the bed be pure'. In Romans 13:3 the same word ('bed') is translated 'sexual immorality'.

3

THE BIG PICTURE

The two will become one flesh. This is a profound mystery – but I am talking about Christ and the church.

St Paul, Ephesians 5:31-32

Marriage ... is an honourable estate ... signifying unto us the mystical union that is betwixt Christ and his church.

Marriage service in the Book of Common Prayer (1549)

We love living in London. There are lots of reasons for that, but one of the best is the easy access to concerts that we enjoy because we live just a couple of Underground stops from the centre of London. Watching any concert is a fascinating thing, but we especially love classical music played by orchestras. As you watch a piece being played, it is possible to be totally absorbed with one particular instrumentalist. You can become fixed on their expression as they play their heart out. You can be increasingly amazed at the dexterity with which they play or the feeling they put into every note. It's almost as though the rest of the orchestra fades away as this one performer fills your gaze. Only, of course, they are just one amongst many, and you need all the parts to enjoy the whole.

It can be like that with what the Bible has to say about sex. Reading the pages of Scripture tells us a lot about sex, including lots of good reasons why God designed things the way that He did. It's easy to become fixated on one of those glorious purposes and miss the big thing that God is showing us; the big thing to which all the other purposes for sex point us to. We need to hear the whole symphony, not just a few instruments playing.

Take procreation – what we normally call having children. It's perfectly possible to take this very good reason for godly sex and make it into the only thing we ever think about when it comes to intimacy within marriage. Historically, the church has sometimes been guilty of that; other times individual Christians certainly have. But when we do so, we are elevating one particular purpose of sex within marriage to a higher status than the Scriptures do. Moreover, we are ignoring the big picture that God gives us in the Bible. It's as though you're coming along to a concert with us and only listening to the violin playing. Our aim in this chapter is to zoom out and make sure we hear the big and beautiful sound the orchestra is making.

It's why we are going to devote this one chapter to the main reason God has given us sex: this is the entire orchestra in action. We're going to try to show you how it informs and shapes every other reason. We're also going to show you how forgetting or neglecting this one reason always leads us down wrong paths. In fact, many of the wrong ideas the world (and Christians too!) has about sex come because we've ignored this big-picture thinking.

GLORY, GLORY, HALLELUJAH

Now, we could of course say that the big purpose of sex is for the glory of God. That must be right because everything is ultimately for His glory. Indeed, this is the way two very good books begin. One – on the subject of sex – is by Denny Burk:

> So what is the purpose of sex? If we clear away all the subordinate purposes, we find that the ultimate purpose of sex is the glory of God. Sex, gender, marriage, manhood, womanhood – all of it – exist ultimately for the glory of God.[1]

That's not just Burk dreaming things up. Neither is he just making a general statement about how everything is for God's glory (for example, from 1 Cor. 10:31). No, he shows clearly in his book, from 1 Corinthians 6, that 'Paul explicitly connects human sexuality with the glory of God.'[2] John Piper's book on marriage makes a similar point, expressed more broadly about marriage:

---

1. Burk, p. 26.
2. Ibid. p. 43.

> The ultimate thing to see in the Bible about marriage is that it exists for God's glory. Most foundationally, marriage is the doing of God. Most ultimately, marriage is the display of God. It is designed by God to display his glory in a way that no other event or institution does.[3]

Piper, as you would expect, then argues his statement biblically.

OK. That doesn't seem like rocket science. It's not just that everything needs to be done for the glory of God (which it does). It is that marriage itself (and sex is part of that equation, as we're about to see) has a particular place in the proclamation of the glory of God. But how? In what way is sex within the marriage relationship – in other words, sex as God has made it – a display of God's glory?

THE MARRIAGE PHOTO

To answer that question we need to take one step back. In what way is *marriage* for God's glory? If we can answer that, we will be some way to answering our questions about sex. The solution is found in Ephesians 5. Paul's epistle to the Ephesians is a wonderfully concise theological and pastoral letter. It contains wonderful teaching about what it means to be in Christ and the applications that necessarily flow out of that reality. Included in these are implications for husbands, wives and children, slaves and masters. In chapter 5, Paul has a little (although it is contentious for some!) to say

---

3.   Piper, p.24.

to wives. They must relate to their husbands as the church relates to Christ. There is a hint that in their marriages there is to be, at the very least, some reflection or modelling on a greater relationship.

> Wives, submit yourselves to your own husbands as you do to the Lord. For the husband is the head of the wife as Christ is the head of the church, his body, of which he is the Saviour (Eph. 5:22-23).

That hint is carried over into the longer instructions that Paul gives the guys:

> Husbands, love your wives, just as Christ loved the church and gave himself up for her to make her holy, cleansing her by the washing with water through the word (Eph. 5:25).

Why, in both cases, does Paul use the relationship between Christ and the church as a model for how husbands and wives are to relate to one another? He doesn't do this for any of the other groups: children, for example, or masters. Something is going on when it comes to marriage and it becomes clear just a few verses on. There Paul returns to our by now familiar Genesis quote, but he adds a twist:

> 'For this reason, a man will leave his father and mother and be united to his wife, and the two will become one flesh.' This is a profound mystery – but I am talking about Christ and the church (Eph. 5:31-32).

Do you see what he is doing? Remarkably, the marriage union depicts a greater reality: that of the relationship between Christ and His church, those chosen in Him before the creation of the world (Eph. 1:4) and redeemed through His blood.

MAKING A PROMISE

This relationship – between Christ and His church – is profoundly important. The Bible calls it a covenant – a technical Bible word for a significant promise or agreement. These covenants in the Bible (of which there are many) are more than occasional details in the story. They *are* the story. From the beginning, God is the God of promise or covenant. And He is also the one who keeps the covenants He makes. He does not break them: He is faithful.

If it is true that marriage reflects the joining of Christ and the church, we should expect the same kind of covenant language to be used for marriage. And it is – both implicitly in the way in which marriage is described and also explicitly, for example in the last book of the Old Testament. Through His prophet, Malachi, God challenges the unfaithfulness of His people and explains that their lack of fidelity is the very reason He has refused to accept their offerings:

> It is because the Lord is the witness between you and the wife of your youth. You have been unfaithful to her, though she is your partner, the wife of your marriage *covenant* (Mal. 2:14, italics added).

There it is in black and white. Paul's words to the Ephesians suddenly don't seem quite so surprising. The marriage relationship between a husband and wife is described in exactly the same terms that God uses to describe His own relationship with His people: covenant. It's not just that marriage relationships bear some resemblance to the joining of Christ and the church as though there is some kind of loose connection. No, the connection is intimate. Paul is clear: the one flesh union between a man and a woman is a clear and profound picture of the union between Christ and the church.

SAME OLD, SAME OLD

This direct picture language should not surprise us as Bible readers, because the same theme has run throughout the Old Testament, except in slightly more indirect language. Time after time, the Lord compares the relationship He has to His people (in the Old Testament, this is expressed in terms of Israel) to that of a marriage. It's a theme that occurs again and again. Indeed, it is nigh on impossible to grasp the Bible story without understanding this truth that underpins it.

That relationship is expressed both positively and negatively in Ezekiel 16. Ezekiel is a prophet who speaks God's words to God's people around the time of the Exile. The line of kings from David has finally proved to be a disaster. God's rebellious people are taken off into Babylon and the word of the Lord through Ezekiel in chapter 16 gives some indication of the way the Lord views everything that has happened. The Lord likens Israel to a young girl that He nurtured and cared for. He does that through childhood and then puberty (v. 7). When the girl is old enough to be married, the Lord covers her and promises to make her His own. That marriage is consummated in the most tender of ways:

> I spread the corner of my garment over you and covered your naked body. I gave you my solemn oath and entered into a covenant with you, declares the Sovereign Lord, and you became mine. I bathed you with water and washed the blood from you and put ointments on you (Ezek. 16:8-9).

What is being described here is effectively the metaphorical wedding night between the Lord and His people. It is remarkably intimate language. However, suddenly the tone of the chapter changes at verse 15, which begins with a very significant 'but'. Israel does not, in essence, remain faithful to her bridegroom, the Lord. Her infidelity is described using some of the most graphic language of the Old Testament:

> At every street corner you built your lofty shrines and degraded your beauty, spreading your legs with increasing promiscuity to anyone who passed by. You engaged in prostitution with the Egyptians, your neighbours with large genitals, and aroused my anger with your increasing promiscuity (Ezek. 16:25-26).

Israel has slept around, attracted not by covenant faithfulness, care and compassion, but by whoever seems to be the most powerful and attractive (here alluded to in terms of sexual appearance: 'large genitals'). The point we want to see, however, is well made. The Lord is the bridegroom and His people are His bride.

JESUS SAYS 'I DO'

This picture is made stronger when we think of the words of Jesus. It's a continuation of the Old Testament for the New to describe Him as the Bridegroom, as happens on many occasions (for example, six times in Matthew, twice each in Mark and Luke, four times in John). 'The bride belongs to the bridegroom' John the Apostle reports his namesake, John the Baptist, as saying (John 3:29), a theme John will again pick up in the awesome verses from the penultimate chapter of the Bible:

> One of the seven angels who had the seven bowls full of the seven last plagues came and said to me, 'Come, I will show you the bride, the wife of the Lamb.' And he carried me away in the Spirit to a mountain great and high, and showed me the Holy City, Jerusalem, coming down out of heaven from God. It shone with the glory of God, and its brilliance was like that of a very precious jewel, like a jasper, clear as crystal (Rev. 21:9-11).

The Old Testament teaches it. Jesus repeats it. The Apostles emphasise it. Here then is marriage as a mysterious picture of a profound truth: it shows us the relationship that Christ has with His people.

JOINED TO JESUS ...

What, though, does it show us about that relationship precisely? It's possible, of course, to liken many things to marriage. My car is like my marriage, goes the old joke, still going after ten years, but not quite the runner it once was. Similes (something is like something else) prove nothing, however. Just because one particular thing is *like* another particular thing doesn't necessarily tell you a whole lot about it, even though it may tell you *something*. We hope you can see, however, that we've got something more than a simile here. The Lord does not say, my relationship with you is *like* a marriage. He says it *is* a marriage. Jesus is not *like* a Bridegroom. He *is* the Bridegroom.

Theologians call this relationship *union with Christ* and Christians down the ages have always understood that's what marriage points towards. That's why we quoted that old Prayer Book line from the marriage service at the beginning of the chapter. Go back and read it now, having read what you've just read.

Union with Christ is a much neglected doctrine. It is central to the Bible's thinking and the teaching of the Apostles. We tend, however, to reduce Christianity down to 'being forgiven' or 'being saved' or 'filled with the Spirit' or 'equipped to serve'. All these are right and good, of course. But they reflect a larger truth which is that – as God's people – we have been made one with Christ for all eternity. This is a way of describing the entirety of what it means to be a believer. As one theologian has put it:

> Union with Christ is not to be understood as a 'moment' in the application of salvation to believers. Rather, it is a way of speaking about the way in which believers share with Christ in eternity (by election), in past history (by redemption), in the present (by effectual calling, justification, and sanctification) and in the future (by glorification).[4]

It's beyond the scope of this little book to go into too much more detail about union with Jesus. However, that's what every marriage reflects. And sex plays an important part in that picture.

ANOTHER MARRIAGE PHOTO

We saw in the last chapter how the one-flesh marriage language includes the sexual intimacy that a wedded couple enjoy. Adam and Eve were 'naked and not ashamed'. In fact, we can go a little further. When God makes Eve she is described by Adam in the most tender of ways:

> This is now bone of my bones and flesh of my flesh; she shall be called 'woman' for she was taken out of man.(Gen. 2:23).

Adam recognises that Eve is taken from him so that they are two separate individuals, each with their own identity. But in some way, marriage reverses this separation. In creation, Eve is flesh of

---

4. Horton, M., *The Christian Faith* (Grand Rapids, Michigan: Zondervan, 2011), p.587.

Adam's flesh – from him but separate from him. Now, in marriage, they are 'one flesh'. There is a re-unification that is more than, but not less than, physical intimacy.

Paul recognises this because he uses the Genesis 2 quote to make an argument against sleeping with a prostitute. The Corinthian Christians, though gloriously saved, had got lots of things wrong. In particular, the world had got into the church and there was a liberality that had spilt into sexual behaviour. 'I have the right to do anything' they claimed (1 Cor. 6:12) including, it appears, sleeping with a prostitute. Paul is rightly aghast.

> Shall I take the members of Christ and unite them with a prostitute? Never! Do you not know that he who unites himself with a prostitute is one with her in body? For it is said, 'The two will become one flesh' (1 Cor. 6:15-16).

Do you recognise our old friend Genesis 2 again? And do you notice how Paul uses the argument of being joined to Christ to argue against this immorality? Christians are 'members of Christ'. They are joined to Him and so cannot become one flesh with the prostitute. Paul's argument is clear: one flesh intimacy is only for marriage; it is the ultimate expression of the union. 'It effects a union that is designed to be an image of Christ's marriage to his bride the church.'[5]

---

5. Burk, p.35.

Sexual intimacy within marriage (in other words, in its proper context) is the closest thing we can get to understanding the depth, profundity, intimacy, closeness, oneness and unity that Jesus' people (the church) enjoy with Him. Let's put it another way. When a couple enjoy the pleasures and delights of sex (a temporary gift for this world), they get a clear picture of the pleasures and delights of being Christ's for all eternity.

There is lots we could say about being one-flesh: sharing a home, passions, delights, joys, children and so on. But within this picture, sex is the ultimate expression of the union.[6] That's pretty awesome! It makes sex, for some at least, a lot *more* important than they have made it: this is how couples can understand something of the unity we have with Christ and the joy and pleasure that springs from it. When sex is reduced to something that married couples perform and little more, we are missing out on the glories of what God has given us.

We would have to say, however, that for others, it makes sex a lot *less* important than they have made it. For these couples, sex is everything, perhaps even an idol, and they have failed to understand it is a great gift to point to an even greater joy.

This part of the drama has an audience of three: husband, wife and God, who sees all. Here the players of the drama watch as they are carried

---

6. It is still an expression of the union, not the union itself. A man who sleeps with a prostitute does not become married to her. Nor does a marriage which becomes sexless cease to be a marriage.

along on currents of pleasure. And if they would honour the meaning of this gift, they will marvel that this – even this, intense as it may be – is by an emblem of something infinitely greater to come.[7]

Sexual union is the ultimate wedding snap, even though it's one married couples keep to themselves.

SEX AND MARRIAGE, HORSE AND CARRIAGE

In the last chapter we saw how many of the Bible's expressions for what we're calling sex (rather coldly, perhaps) imply a context. It is noticeable, in fact, that there aren't really Bible words which equate to our modern expression 'to have sex'. There is no cold, mechanical description. We can now be a bit more specific: that context is marriage. How do we know? We know because there is an order and containment in marriage:

> That is why a man leaves his father and mother and is united to his wife, and they become one flesh. Adam and his wife were both naked, and they felt no shame (Gen 2:24-25).

The order is obvious. This verse describes a prototype marriage. A man leaves his parental home to be joined to his wife. They are married: 'they become one flesh.' The one-flesh union of which sexual intimacy is the ultimate expression follows. This order may be slow (it may take many months of courtship and so on). Or it may be relatively speedy. It all depends on the circumstances and

---

7.   Piper, pp.128-9.

culture. Martin Luther got engaged early in the eve-
ning, married straight afterwards and his marriage
was consummated later that night, with witnesses![8]
Perhaps not many (any?) of us experience or hope
for that kind of speed. Nevertheless, even Martin's
strange courtship follows the same pattern.

However, there is also containment. The marriage is the *place* for sexual intimacy. This foundational truth is made clear in the Scriptures because
when sexual intimacy takes place outside of marriage (often called 'adultery' or 'marital unfaithfulness') the marriage may be ended. Under the Old
Testament law the end of the marriage might come
by punishment (death for either offending partner). It may also come through divorce.

What this means is that marriage and sex belong together. They are so closely linked that it
seems that at times the Bible writers treat them as
the same thing, even though one is an expression
of another. For example, when some of the proph-
ets speak about breaking marriage covenants, they
sometimes do it in terms of covenant, marriage
and divorce language (Mal. 2 would be a good
example). They also do it in terms of sexual fidelity and infidelity (Ezek. 16 is perhaps the best
example).

We do the same in much of modern speech. We
might talk about 'Washington' meaning the United
States of America. 'Washington has passed a law ...',

---

8. Cited by Justin Taylor in Piper, J. & Taylor, J., *Sex and the Supremacy of Christ* (Wheaton, Illinois: Crossway Books, 2005), p.222.

we might say, for example. Washington is not the U.S. It is a part of it, an expression of it – but the two are so closely connected, that when we talk in this way, people understand what we are saying. Sex and marriage share this kind of connection.

Some commentators like to say that this is because sex is the covenant sign, much like baptism is a sign of the new covenant.[9] We do agree that marriage is a covenant (as we've already seen). But we're not fully persuaded by the 'sign' argument which seems to be extrapolated from Scripture rather than being explicit there (and strangely absent, if it is true). In one sense, it doesn't matter too much; what we can say with great Bible assurance is that the connection is close, very close indeed: marriage is the place for sex and sex is for marriage. They go together like, well, a horse and carriage. It's no surprise then that the two are used almost interchangeably.

... AND JESUS TO THE FATHER
There's one more thing to say about this big picture, however. The language of oneness is important in the Scriptures. We saw it there in Genesis 2:24. We've now seen that Christ and the church are one. But there's another oneness that runs through the pages of the Bible. It's the oneness enjoyed by the three persons of the Trinity: Father, Son and Holy Spirit. They are separate persons, yet one indivisible Unity.

---

9. This is Michael Lawrence's argument in Piper & Taylor (ibid.), p.137-8.

Christians down the ages have struggled to find ways to explain this satisfactorily. Most descriptions, it turns out, tend to make you into some kind of ancient heretic. Ever heard that the Trinity is like H_2O? It exists in three different forms – ice, water, and steam. That's – if you're interested – the heresy of Modalism: that the Father, the Son and the Holy Spirit are three forms of one God. Or what about the one where God is like the sun? The Father is the star, the Son the light it brings, the Spirit the heat it delivers. Ever heard that one? That's – again, if you're interested – the heresy of Arianism: that the Son and Spirit are creations of the greater Father.

Nope, it's pretty difficult to explain the Trinity. We can say, however, what we see in the Bible. God is One yet three distinct persons, Father, Son and Holy Spirit. How can that be? How is it possible for three to be one at the same time? Earthly analogies – like those two we've just described – are hopeless. But what about this: what if there was some thing or some experience where two distinct persons who remain distinct and two also function as one? You can perhaps see where this is leading. The two of Genesis 2:24 become one flesh. They don't stop being husband and wife. They are always male and female. And yet these two become mysteriously and gloriously one as the husband joins himself to his wife in one flesh.

If this seems a bit far-fetched, the connection between union with Christ (or, in fact, God) and the church *and* the relationships that exist within the eternal Trinity is a link that Jesus Himself makes in His high-priestly prayer. Jesus prays for unity amongst His followers, praying that they may be one:

> ... just as you are in me and I am in you: [Trinity] May they also be in us [union] so that the world may believe that you have sent me (John 17:21).

It is possible to overstate this point, of course. Husband and wife are two who become one. The Trinity is, well, a trinity. But the point carries some truth. As husband and wife experience the close oneness of sexual intimacy, they not only experience the intensity of the marriage covenant and point towards the greater truth (Christ and the church), but they also learn and discover something of the very nature of God Himself.[10]

What a picture!

SORTING RIGHT FROM WRONG
You may never have thought about sexual intimacy in this way. But it is important to do so, and not just because the Scriptures do. You see, if we can get the real fundamentals right, we're more likely to understand the moral implications. For many outside the church, their view of Christianity and sex is as a list of do's and don'ts. Mostly don'ts, to be honest. People think that all Christians are interested in, is drawing boundaries more tightly than the world does.

---

10. We're grateful to our colleague Tim Ward for helping us to see this more clearly.

Now, there is *some* truth in that. God's Word is clear about some of the sexual boundaries that should and must exist. Most famously, perhaps, this is expressed in the seventh commandment: 'you shall not commit adultery'. And if you were to read on into the law, both in Exodus and other law books such as Leviticus and Deuteronomy, you would find plenty of those 'boundary' commands and rules.

But having seen the big picture allows us to do three things. First, it allows sex to be the proclamation that God intended it to be. It is not, of course, a public proclamation in the sense that it is viewed by the world. Sex is appropriately private. Nonetheless, as the church proclaims this big picture in a positive and biblical way, it proclaims something of the relationship between Christ and the church. This is most true of a Christian view of marriage, but it is also true of the particular sexual expression of marriage. As Christians stand for fidelity, we proclaim Christ's fidelity. Too often we are on the back foot debating what Christians may or may not do. If only we can reclaim something of the deep significance of this marital intimacy, then we would be able to be pro-actively positive in proclaiming the truths to which it points.

Secondly, understanding this big picture allows us to understand precisely why boundaries are so important. They themselves are not simply the rules of a fun-hating God (as the caricature is sometimes portrayed). No – they are obvious and necessary applications for a crucial truth regarding the very nature of the salvation relationship: Christ and His church. In other words, seeing the big picture helps us see beyond lists of rules and regulations.

And, thirdly, seeing the big picture allows us to work these things out from first principles. We need that because in our world of changing sexual mores, we're always being challenged by new situations and changed circumstances about which the Bible might not say anything specific. Knowing the underlying truths will help us get sexual morality right every time. Take the seventh commandment. This law on adultery is crystal clear. It would be perfectly possible, however, to work it out anyway, even if it were not given to us. The argument goes something like this: Christ and His church have and enjoy an exclusively intimate relationship. You cannot be saved outside of Christ and you need Christ for continuing in salvation. It's pretty simple, really.

And, therefore, the picture must reflect the reality. Sexual intimacy outside of marriage implies that the exclusivity which Christ and the church enjoy is also negotiable (Paul's very point in 1 Cor. 6). Put more simply, if one of us is allowed to sleep with whom we want, irrespective of our marriage commitments, then an exclusive relationship with Christ is also unnecessary. Put more bluntly, if it is OK to sleep around, then it is OK to be unfaithful to Christ. Or, to express it in a more biblical way: because Christ demands and deserves our unfailing faithfulness, so our spouses – and they alone – rightly demand and deserve unfailing sexual faithfulness.

Yes, this truly is an amazing picture that God has given couples.

> Marriage at its exquisite peak of pleasure speaks powerfully the truth of covenant-keeping love between Christ and his church.[11]

This truth is worth meditating over and reflecting on. It makes sex – already wondrously good – something of even greater import. The implications of it are worked out throughout the pages of Scripture, and that's now where we turn.

---

11. Piper, p.135.

4

So much more

The husband should fulfil his marital duty to his wife, and
likewise the wife to her husband. The wife does not have
authority over her own body but yields it to her husband. In
the same way, the husband does not have authority over his
own body but yields it to his wife. Do not deprive each other
except perhaps by mutual consent and for a time, so that you
may devote yourselves to prayer. Then come together again
so that Satan will not tempt you because of your lack of self-
control.   *St Paul, 1 Corinthians 7:3-5*

Celebration is not optional for the married. We are commanded to enjoy each other's bodies.   *John Piper*[1]

We've now seen that there is a big picture within which sex must be understood – nothing
less, in fact, than as a private expression of an extraordinary reality: we, the church, the bride of
Christ are intimately joined to Him in an everlasting unbreakable union. It is this big picture which
informs our understanding of much to do with sex.
That the Bible says more about sex than this, does

---

1.   Piper, J., *This Momentary Marriage* (Nottingham: Inter-Varsity Press,
     2009), p.128.

not diminish this big picture. In fact, we've begun to see how pretty much everything the Bible says about sex could be derived from this one principle. For example, as we've just seen, the command to marital faithfulness is not just because monogamy is important in itself (though, sociologically, it is). It is because any deviation from a monogamous married lifestyle destroys the picture.

However, it is also true that the Bible does say other things about sex and they are worth reviewing. These are subsidiary to our big point, but no less important for it. And it may surprise some that the Bible has such a broad and positive view. Indeed, as the world has become more liberal about the practice and talk of sex in the last fifty years, the church has often responded (albeit unwittingly) by presenting a negative view of sex: we have often concentrated on what is not acceptable (understandably so) rather than what is good and holy.

Please hear us correctly: that view is sometimes right. As we have already seen, when it comes to sex, context matters a lot. What is pure, holy, joyful and delightful in the right setting can be impure, immoral, shameful and plain wrong in another. Context is everything – which is why the previous chapter is so important.

But given that sex takes place in the context of a proper marriage, as the Bible understands it, we can be remarkably positive about it. If we have understood that marriage is primarily a depiction of the union Christ has with the church expressed supremely in sex, we can downshift a little and now say here are five other purposes for the God-given delight of sexual union between a husband and wife.[2]

SEX IS FOR PARTNERSHIP

Sex is the best and God-given way to express the partnership that husband and wife share. Nothing else comes close to doing that. Couples can have joint bank accounts; wives can change their names; they can hold hands in public and go on holiday together. In fact, they should perhaps do *all* of these things! But nothing expresses union like sex. There's an important principle at stake here:

> So God created mankind in his own image, in the image of God he created them, male and female he created them (Gen. 1:27).

God creates mankind (singular, in Hebrew *adam*, a word which is a noun meaning man or mankind, but which becomes the proper name of God's first creation, Adam). There is an equality about this creation, even though the verse then expressly distinguishes between men and women: 'male and female he created them.' Here we have the heart of the Bible's teaching about humanity, namely,

---

2. Other writers come up with similar lists, a not altogether surprising fact when one simply surveys the Bible literature. Closest to our list is that of Feinberg & Feinberg, *Ethics for a Brave New World 2ⁿᵈ Edition* (Wheaton, Illinois: Crossway Books, 2010), pp. 302-304. An alternative approach (more thoughtful and involved) is that taken by our colleague Christopher Ash (ibid., pp. 103-131) who evaluates the 'procreational good', the 'relational good' and the 'public good' in the context of the foundational texts of Genesis 1–2.

we are created equally in God's image, but with fundamental differences.

Now let's leap onto the next chapter. In chapter 2 we get a little more detail of how verse 27 of chapter 1 came about. We see Adam being presented with all the animals to see whether any are able to assist him in the work of stewardship that will be given to mankind. 'But for Adam no suitable helper was found' (v. 20). None of the animals could be the partner that Adam needed. So, God causes Adam to fall into a deep sleep and Eve is created from Adam's flesh. This first woman comes from the first man. To put it another way, Eve is, before her creation, part of Adam. Hence, her name:

> The man said, 'This is now bone of my bones and flesh of my flesh; she shall be called "woman" for she was taken out of man.' That is why a man leaves his father and mother and is united to his wife, and they become one flesh (Gen. 2:23-24).

Can you see how the circle is completed? Eve comes from Adam, but in marriage is joined to him again as his equal partner. It is this physical *re*-uniting (if we can call it that) that will create future men and women, who themselves will be joined, and so on and so forth. We believe it is going too far to say – as some do – that sex is an antidote to the loneliness that Adam must obviously feel. There's no indication that he is *lonely*. It is simply that no suitable helper can be found. He does not need a partner to help pass the long evenings. He needs a partner to help fulfil the creation mandate.

So, we don't want to say sex is an antidote to loneliness. But we do want to say that sexual intimacy within marriage is an expression of the partnership that God gives husband and wife that can be expressed in no better way.

Interestingly, Christians are sometimes shy today of using the word 'partner'. It has been rather hi-jacked by the world to describe someone with whom you live, but who is not married to you. It's a way of normalising that kind of cohabiting relationship. But it is first and foremost a Bible word: Proverbs 2:17 uses it to describe a husband. In the last book of the Old Testament, Malachi, the Lord addresses the nation's unfaithfulness both to Him and to their marriages. He will no longer look with favour upon them:

> You ask, 'Why?' It is because the LORD is the witness between you and the wife of your youth. You have been unfaithful to her, though she is your partner, the wife of your marriage covenant (Mal. 2:14).

In the Greek version of the Old Testament (that Jesus and Paul knew), the word translated 'partner' here is the word that is often translated 'fellowship' in the New Testament. We tend to think fellowship means spending time together. After church, we sometimes say there will be 'times of fellowship'. But the word is deeper than that. It means to share *in* something *with* somebody. It is appropriately used of church relationships. The Greek translation was right to translate Malachi 2 in this way. In fact,

Paul expresses the same idea negatively. In 2 Corinthians 6 he urges the Christians to be careful whom they partner with:

> Do not be yoked together with unbelievers. For what do righteousness and wickedness have in common? Or what fellowship [or partnership] can light have with darkness (2 Cor. 6:14).

This is not, primarily, an instruction about whom Christians can marry, as we have sometimes made it. It is a broader principle. Nevertheless, it would include marriage principles and carries over that Old Testament idea that marriage is about partnership. Sex, we argue, is the most potent expression of that togetherness. Of course, it is a private expression. Unlike almost anything else, it is not something that anybody else but the married couple see or experience. There are no cameras in the bedroom. It is for private consumption only. However, it still stands as an intense depiction of the partnership that should pervade the marriage. There is an equality about sex which reflects the equality that exists within marriage – different roles, for sure (hopefully, that's obvious to anybody with a rudimentary understanding of the body). But equality nonetheless:

> The husband should fulfil his marital duty to his wife, and likewise the wife to her husband. The wife does not have authority over her own body, but yields it to her husband. In the same way, the husband does not have authority over his own body, but yields it to his wife (1 Cor 7:3-4).

We must also see that for this partnership to be genuine it must be two-way. This is one of the most radical things we can say about sex. It is a service to the other partner. It is about 'yielding' to the other, to use Paul's vocabulary. Most people today are interested in whether something is good for them. That is their message of success. 'Did it do *me* good?' is the key question. Christians, in this area and others, ask quite a different question. 'Did it do *you* good?' That's how Christian partnership works.

Sex, then, expresses this partnership *emotionally*, as perhaps nothing else can. However, there is more than an emotional fellowship. The partnership is practical too because this most private and intimate of actions is the God-ordained way that God's command to mankind is fulfilled, which brings us neatly to our next principle.

SEX IS FOR PROCREATION

It may seem like we're stating the obvious, but sex is for procreation or, to put it more colloquially, for making babies. It is worth spending just a little time on this for two reasons. First, we live in a world where, increasingly, it is considered normal (or at least not particularly extraordinary) to conceive a child by artificial means. This is not the place to consider the various moral issues raised by artificially conceived children (for example, where a fertilised egg is implanted in a woman's uterus). Suffice it to say, it is technologically possible and often – in the world's eyes – morally permissible too. In a world where conception can happen in other ways, we may be tempted to forget that God's design for procreation is that it is a consequence of sexual intercourse.

Secondly, we can be too reductionist about sex and make it just about making babies. These days such views are increasingly uncommon, but this was a particular battle the Reformers fought and is still found in the writings of some of the early church leaders.

> The Protestant Reformation began against the backdrop of a Roman Catholic Church that valued virginity above marriage. Prudery very much characterized the Roman Catholic disposition towards sex. Many in the Roman church believed you could not have sex without sinning, even with your spouse.[3]

We hope that reading this little book will give you a broader view of sex. Nevertheless, it is not just stating the obvious to link sex with procreation. Indeed, this is how the Bible begins with humanity.

> So God created mankind in his own image, in the image of God he created them; male and female he created them. God blessed them and said to them, 'Be fruitful and increase in number; fill the earth and subdue it. Rule over the fish in the sea and the birds in the sky and over every living creature that moves on the ground' (Gen. 1:27-28).

---

3. Mark Dever, writing in Piper, J., & Taylor, J., *Sex and the Supremacy of Christ* (Wheaton, Illinois: Crossway, 2005), p.247.

Right from the start, when God creates man and woman, He gives them a job to do. That job is to rule as His regent over the creation He has made. That role is flagged up from the beginning when Adam and Eve were both created in God's image, which is to somehow take on some of the attributes of God in the world He spoke into being. The command to be fruitful and increase in number (to have children, in other words) should not be read independently of the command to fill the earth and subdue it. How is mankind to rule over everything God has made (v. 28)? That's a lot of animals. And a lot of fields. Even pre-Fall, that is an enormous task. Animals will multiply too. God is not giving the first couple a little petting zoo to oversee. He is giving them the world!

The only way that the command to rule can be fulfilled is if the earth is filled with offspring. Thus, the Lord speaks the word of procreation to Mr and Mrs Adam. 'Be fruitful and increase in number'. Many reasons are given today why couples should have children. At one extreme, some argue that Christian couples should have as many children as possible. Can that be right? Well, one way to answer this vexed question is to go back to Genesis 1 and see the original reason couples were commanded to procreate – it was to fulfil the creation mandate. It was, in other words, to serve God.[4]

Decisions whether to have children or not, and how many, are difficult for many couples. There are

---

4. This is essentially the point that Ash (ibid.) makes in his book, though he does it more eloquently and comprehensively than we have done here.

all sorts of issues involved, not least the incredible pain that some couples face when they discover they are unable to have children. Nevertheless, it seems to us that the plain reading of Scripture is that this is one of the reasons that God has given couples the gift of sex. It is precisely so that they can reproduce. Indeed, if sex is for partnership with each other, perhaps we can also express it like this: sex is also for partnership *with God* to fulfil the original command He gives in Genesis 1:28.

For what it's worth, we think many of the answers about whether to have children, how many, and when, are found in understanding this original mandate. The procreation element of sex is closely linked to the command that God gives Adam and Eve, and therefore making godly and wise decisions about children – if we are able – should also be done in the context of how that command is fulfilled today.[5] Why, however, did God design procreation the way that he did? Luther famously quipped:

> The reproduction of mankind is a great marvel and mystery. Had God consulted me in the matter, I should have advised him to continue the generation of the species by fashioning them of clay, in the way Adam was fashioned.[6]

---

5. There is a very helpful and pastoral chapter expanding on this theme in Ash, C., *Married for God* (Nottingham: IVP Books, 2007), pp.49-63.

6. Luther, M., *Table Talk* (Albany, Oregon: Books for the Ages, 1997), p.329. Originally published as *Divine Discourses*.

The Lord did not consult Martin, however. And, we might say, a good thing too.

SEX IS FOR PLEASURE

Sex is fun. Good. Pleasurable. Enjoyable. Delightful. For sure, that is not true for every couple all of the time. We all of us who are married have seasons where sex – for many different reasons – is painful (physically and emotionally), less than good or simply non-existent. We don't want to diminish the troubles that some couples have (and we urge you – if that is you – to seek some help). But neither should the exceptions discolour the overall truth. Sex is pleasurable. That is the way God has made it.

Presumably, God didn't *have* to make it that way. There is no question that God could have designed humanity with a different way of procreating. He could have taken Luther's advice. Or He could, at least, have made us more like the animal kingdom where, very often, mating is a cursory, quick, mechanical process. But He did not. Of course, the fact that something is pleasurable in itself does not prove anything. Sin is sometimes pleasurable in the moment – that's why we disobey God and follow our own paths. But in this case, our point is backed up by Scripture. As Solomon advises:

> May your fountain be blessed,
> and may you rejoice in the wife of your youth.
> A loving doe, a graceful deer –
> may her breasts satisfy you always,
> may you ever be intoxicated with her love
> (Prov. 5:18-19).

In fact, there is a whole Bible book devoted to this subject: Song of Songs (or, as it is sometimes called The Song of Solomon). Now before we get to look at some of what this book says, we need to pause and consider the book as a whole. That's because Christians over hundreds of years have sometimes shied away from saying that the book is about a relationship between a man and a woman. If you've ever read Song of Songs, you may be surprised to hear that. The language is surprisingly and obviously graphic and you can't help wondering whether some of the more guarded language is actually a kind of ancient code for things (or body parts!) that are even more explicit.

Some of our forefathers found this language a little, shall we say, difficult? And so, like many parts of the Old Testament, they allegorised the book. Allegory is seeing what is written not as a description of what it appears to be, but a picture of something else. On this basis, they said, Song of Songs is depicting the relationship between the Bride and the Bridegroom: between the church and Christ. This allegory was sometimes taken to – it might seem – ridiculous levels. For example, regarding the wife's breasts in 4:5:

> Some apply these to the two Testaments; others to the two sacraments, the seals of the covenant of grace; others to ministers, who are to be spiritual nurses to the children of God and to give out to them the sincere milk of the word, that they may grow thereby, and, in order to that, are themselves

to feed among the lilies where Christ feeds, that they may be to the babes of the church as full breasts. [7]

Before you scoff too much at this interpretation (perhaps, we admit, encouraged by what we've just written), there *is* some truth in this. If it is true that sexual intimacy within a marriage context is an expression of the covenant relationship between Christ and His church, then it follows that a Bible book about a sexual marriage relationship is ultimately about precisely that subject. Our forefathers were, at one level, correct. In the scramble to reclaim Song of Songs as a book about what it appears to be, we have to be careful to say our biblical theology demands that it is *more* than a book about sex. However, it is not less than that. As C.J. Mahaney puts it:

> Spiritualizing the Song of Solomon just doesn't make sense. What's worse, it denies to us the powerful impact that God intends for it to have on our marriages. [8]

It might seem rather a waste of time to prove from the Scriptures that sex is pleasurable. But it's worth doing so because there will always be Christians (and you may be one) who are suspicious that something the world recognises as pleasurable could be

---

7. Henry, M., *Matthew Henry's Commentary on the Whole Bible: Complete and Unabridged in One Volume* (Peabody: Hendrickson, 1994) p. 1065.

8. Mahaney, C.J., *Sex, Romance and the Glory of God* (Wheaton, Illinois: Crossway Books, 2004), p.13.

so for Christians too. We are, rightly perhaps, wary of bringing worldly attitudes into the church. However, it is important to see that understanding sex as pleasurable is not bringing a worldly attitude into the church. God designed sex and purposed it for pleasure. When the world (in whatever setting) recognises sex as enjoyable, it is they are who are taking the Bible into the world, even though that would rarely be acknowledged.

So, back to Song of Songs. Most of the book is a conversation between a man (let's call him Mr Solomon) and a woman, betrothed to him and soon to be his wife. Let's call her Mrs Solomon. We could spend a long time examining the book in detail, but let's just take two quotes to demonstrate the joyful nature of sexual union. Let's start with Mr Solomon.

How beautiful you are, my darling!
Oh, how beautiful!
Your eyes behind your veil are doves.
Your hair is like a flock of goats
descending from the hills of Gilead.
[2] Your teeth are like a flock of sheep just shorn,
coming up from the washing.
Each has its twin;
not one of them is alone.
[3] Your lips are like a scarlet ribbon;
your mouth is lovely.
Your temples behind your veil
are like the halves of a pomegranate.
[4] Your neck is like the tower of David,

built with courses of stone;
on it hang a thousand shields,
all of them shields of warriors.
⁵ Your breasts are like two fawns,
like twin fawns of a gazelle
that browse among the lilies.
⁶ Until the day breaks
and the shadows flee,
I will go to the mountain of myrrh
and to the hill of incense.
⁷ You are altogether beautiful, my darling;
there is no flaw in you (Song 4:1-7).

This is the language of Mr Solomon delighting in his bride, Mrs Solomon. Some of the language may seem slightly obscure. Other parts are, frankly, somewhat ridiculous sounding to our modern ears. Try – fellas – telling your wife tonight that her teeth are like sheep! But though these words are separated from us by thousands of years of culture, we understand them well enough. This is Mr Solomon taking us on a tour of Mrs Solomon's body *and delighting in it*. Sometimes he is clear what he is talking about – there is no coyness speaking about breasts, for example. Other times the language is more guarded and veiled – you can use your imagination to work out what the 'mountain of myrrh' and 'hill of incense' are. For Mr Solomon, the very anticipation of his wife's body is not something to be ashamed of, but rather something to delight in.

You'll be glad to know that the sentiment is reciprocated. Mrs Solomon is also eagerly anticipating their night of consummation. She is sometimes more coy than her fiancé. That is partly because, in the Hebrew culture of the time, breasts could be talked about openly, whereas genitals (male and female) were generally referred to more obliquely. Nevertheless, we can still see a strong sentiment of anticipated pleasure in her. We can see that in the way she responds to Mr Solomon's speech that we have just read:

> Awake, north wind,
> and come, south wind!
> Blow on my garden,
> that its fragrance may spread everywhere.
> Let my beloved come into his garden
> and taste its choice fruits (Song 4:16).

Now, it's quite possible that Mrs Solomon is a keen gardener and she is hoping to impress Mr Solomon with her herb collection. Possible, but unlikely. What's going on here? Mrs Solomon is inviting Mr Solomon into her bed. Not to put too fine a point on it, she wants to make love to him and is offering her perfumed body to him to come, taste and enjoy. The fact that her invitation is couched in rather abstract fruity and gardening terms does not lessen the impact. She wants to sleep with him and longs for him to enjoy the experience, much as a refreshing fruit bowl might invigorate a weary, hungry traveller in a hot country.

It is true that elsewhere in the Bible, sex is sometimes spoken of in more mechanical ways. The language of 'duty' or 'conjugal rights' that we have already seen in 1 Corinthians 7 might perhaps – taken on its own – give the impression that sex is a necessary part of marriage, but hardly enjoyable or pleasurable: a bit like putting out the rubbish. But thankfully we have Song of Songs to correct that notion. Sex is good and pleasurable. God has made it that way. It's fun – most of the time.

SEX IS FOR PEACE-MAKING

We sometimes imagine that sex within marriage is for the good times. It is for the times when both husband and wife are feeling good about life, about their bodies, when they are not tired or exhausted, where there are no unresolved issues, when the children have gone to bed early and so on. On this basis, sex would be a once-a-year celebration! God has wonderfully designed sexual intimacy to be more than this. Yes, there are the swinging-from-the-chandeliers type moments. But there is also what we might call 'vanilla sex' – plain and simple and not requiring two hours pre-booked into the diary. However, sex is not just for the good times either.

Sex is also a comfort. At its best it pacifies. It calms and soothes. It brings peace to situations and relationships. Much like a baby is pacified by having a dummy to suck on, so sex can bring calm and comfort to couples going through the most difficult of circumstances. This is not a kind of one-sided imposition or release of tension: the Bible gives no warrant for such behaviour. Rather, it is the mutual comforting and reconciling that a willing couple benefit from.

Sometimes, when times are tough and sad, couples refrain from sex. That may seem an obvious thing to do. No one wants to watch a comedy on TV having just received news of a relative's death and, in much the same way, people cannot envisage sexual intimacy during times of trial. But there is an intriguing reference to sex in the Bible that gives us a surprising insight into the way God has made things to be.

It comes in the story of David and Bathsheba. To be honest, it's difficult to read this story with a clear head. David is a deep sinner. Not only does he commit adultery with Bathsheba, he arranges for her husband, Uriah, to be killed at the front line (when all his other schemes have failed). Adulterer! Murderer! But we need to understand that the story does resolve itself. David is confronted by the prophet Nathan and repents of his sin. God forgives with one of the most remarkable statements of the whole episode:

> Then David said to Nathan, 'I have sinned against the LORD.' Nathan replied, 'The LORD has taken away your sin. You are not going to die. But because by doing this you have shown utter contempt for the LORD, the son born to you will die' (2 Sam. 12:13-14).

As a response to David's genuine repentance, David's sin is removed by our gracious Lord. From now on, we must read the story in the light of this forgiveness. It is hard not to read on with a distaste in our mouths as we see how David speaks and acts. But from here on in, he is a restored man and we must view his actions positively. Not that everything is rosy in the garden. The son born to Bathsheba becomes ill as a consequence of David's sin and the king pleads with God for him. However, true to the word of the Lord, the boy dies. It is what happens next we want to highlight.

> Then David comforted his wife Bathsheba, and he went to her and made love to her. She gave birth to a son, and they named him Solomon. The LORD loved him (2 Sam. 12:24).

The NIV captures the right sense here because, although the first sentence is describing separate actions ('comforted', 'went' and 'made love') they are all closely connected by conjunctions. Neither is separate from the other. Married couples can perhaps use their experience to imagine what kind of sex this is. Bathsheba's son has just died! This is not the moment for lacy lingerie. Quite the opposite. Words like 'pleasure' and 'fun' hardly seem appropriate. This is most likely quiet, sober sex with tears and sobs.

But that it happens at all is significant. The sexual union of David and Bathsheba (now morally right, because they are forgiven and husband and wife) is a comfort to Bathsheba at least, and probably David too (though the text does not say that explicitly). And this sad, sorrowful coupling is the moment when God's plans are advanced and the great king who will extend David's line is conceived. This moment is the beginning of Solomon.

Given that sex is an expression of the union between Christ and the church we should not be surprised at this purpose. Christ is not just for the good times. We don't feel close to Him only when things are going well. In fact, it is precisely in the difficult trials and troubles that we crave intimacy and closeness with Him.

In our limited experience, this function of sex as a comfort is greatly undervalued by Christians. Anecdotally (we can't prove it statistically), many couples draw apart sexually in crises: sometimes something as traumatic as the death of a child; sometimes something less extreme, but difficult nonetheless: redundancy, for example. The reasons why sex may be difficult in these times are many and varied – loss of self-esteem, for example. But we want to say that this is not the way God has made it to be.

It is precisely in these times of trouble that married couples can comfort one another with the intimacy that God graciously gives to them. It's unlikely to rock the bed. Nor will it change the situations and circumstances we find ourselves in. But for a moment it takes us away from the cares and troubles of the world and provides solace and comfort. It's a gift for just those moments.

SEX IS FOR PROTECTION

Finally, we turn to the passage we've already considered in 1 Corinthians 7. Twice, in this one passage, Paul alludes to the fact that regular sexual intimacy between a husband and a wife guards against moral failure in a sexually pressurised world. The first phrase comes in verse 2:

> *But since sexual immorality is occurring*, each man should have sexual relations with his own wife, and each woman with her own husband. (Italics added)

The protection is made more specific in verse 5:

> Do not deprive each other except perhaps by mutual consent and for a time, so that you may devote yourselves to prayer. Then come together again so that Satan will not tempt you because of your lack of self-control.

The couple who abstain from sex (presumably a 'super-spiritual' approach that some in Corinth were advocating) put themselves at great risk from outside: more particularly, it puts them at risk of satanic attack. The attack has the potential to be effective because of a lack of self-control in us, something that Satan presumably seeks to deliberately expose and exploit. What is this self-control we lack? It must be nothing less than the self-control required to keep our sexual libido under control. Once marriage has kindled that regular desire, removal is a disaster and – in general terms – abstention may well lead us into sin.

This seems a rather harsh verdict from the Apostle. After all, what about the many single people? Are they equally at risk? We take it that this is why in the next sentence Paul expresses a desire that more might be single as he is – but that each needs to exercise the gift given by God Himself. In other words, singleness is a gift as much as marriage. This is an important principle for Paul to make at this point for otherwise there would be little hope for self-control in those who are single. However, if singleness is indeed a gift (literally a *charisma*) then we can expect and trust that God will equip those with the gift for everything they need to serve Him with it.

What are we seeing here? We're seeing that regular sexual activity (and that will mean different things for different couples in different circumstances) is given by God not only to bring pleasure, closeness and children, but to protect from the world in which we live. One thing we can certainly say about twenty-first century Western society is that it is more and more like the Corinthian version. In such a situation it is a great comfort to know that, as husbands and wives celebrate sex, they keep Satan at the door. How so? Paul doesn't expand, but it's not difficult to join the dots. At one level, regular sex (especially for men) removes the desire for sexual release. Put crudely, once a man has enjoyed sex, he's done for a while. He is physically satisfied. For women, the issue is slightly more complex and is linked not just to physical satisfaction, but emotional fulfilment.

But there may be more to Paul's argument than this. After all, he has already been speaking about the deep meaning of sexual intimacy as we saw in the last chapter. He has done this negatively up to this point (dealing with prostitution). But the point is still well made. If Christians understand sex in the big picture we have tried to show, then regular sex stands as a regular reminder of the truth in question. Perhaps if we, as Christians, disciplined ourselves to think this way a little more, it would make a difference to the number of sad and tragic incidences of unfaithfulness within Christian marriages?

If we reduce sex to a pleasure zone and nothing more, we lose sight of this protecting influence. Regular reflection of the big picture when it comes to sex is sensible, godly and useful and will help us avoid Satan's temptations. It does, however, seem a little cold to think about sexual intimacy in this way. After all, 'let's go to bed so Satan can't tempt us' hardly seems a romantic invitation! But, if we understand the deep purpose of God in giving us sex within marriage, it is actually a *very* romantic notion, for it will in God's goodness help preserve the covenant faithfulness that God demands and Christ shows to us in the gospel of grace. As John Piper writes with his poetic flair:

> A married couple give a severe blow to the head of that ancient serpent when they aim to give as much sexual satisfaction to each other as possible.[9]

TAKING A REALITY CHECK

There are all kinds of reasons why sex in marriage is not all that it should be. Perhaps our list of words beginning with P seems a long way from

9.   Piper, p.135.

the reality you experience right at the moment? We need to remember that we're sinners married to sinners and, whilst the Bible holds out to us an ideal, it can sometimes seem a million miles apart from what we know today. If that describes you, don't lose heart! Our struggles in this area do not undermine the purposes we've outlined here and the very important picture we set out in the last chapter. In fact, in our walk with Christ, we feel some of those same ups and downs. That is what it feels like to struggle with our residual sinful nature; but we press on, knowing that one day we shall see Christ face to face and be made like Him.

Similarly in marriage, it will not be a bed of roses all the time. That is as true in the bedroom as it is around the kitchen table. Difficulties do not allow us to jettison the truth which we have been considering. In fact, it is that very truth which gives us something to aim for. If sex seems humdrum, routine, difficult or even non-existent, then as Christians we have a good corrective to implement. It is not a book of techniques or a self-help DVD. First and foremost it is that God has given this good gift in marriage for a purpose. And it is meditating on this purpose, praying about it, reflecting on it that will help transform our thinking.

Christ loves His church. He died for her. By the Holy Spirit He is joined to her. He preserves her. He protects her. He comforts her. And knowing these truths should help every married Christian to rejoice in the private portrait He has granted to each of us.

5
WHAT IF ...?

Marriage should be honoured by all and the marriage bed kept pure.

Hebrews 13:4

We never intended this short introductory book to be a 'how to' manual, nor for it to address particular issues in detail. Nevertheless, given all that we have said so far, it would be pastorally remiss of us not to identify some issues that do arise. We'll do no more here than briefly discuss each issue and direct you to other resources that you may find useful. But please don't let issues fester under the surface and destroy relationships. We hope you've been able to see that this is an important subject and fixing things that are wrong is part of the work God always wants to do in us, as He transforms us into the likeness of His Son.

WHAT IF ... I'M SINGLE?

All this talk of sex can be hard for singles to take. The relatively recent freedom which Christians feel in expressing themselves about sex compounds the issue. Frankly, it was much easier when the minister was too embarrassed to talk about sex from the front at church. Now he's saying how great it is! How does that help singles? Those who preach and teach must bear some responsibility for the insensitivity that is sometimes shown to those who are single. Married preachers are particularly susceptible to getting so carried away that they neglect to think about how what they say affect those to whom they are speaking. Some correction here would be welcome!

But here is the greatest truth of all. Sexual intimacy in its right and proper context (within marriage) is only a picture of something much, much better. This truth – which we've tried to show you in this book – needs to set the context for all talk in church about sex. When it does not, the church is in danger of doing exactly what the world does – making sex into an idol. However, set in its proper context, sex points us towards a greater reality. And the greatest truth of all is that, with or without sex, every Christian knows and experiences that reality.

Let us put it like this. As a single person, you may feel like you're missing out on sex. But in fact you, together with every Christian, have the greater, more beautiful, more awesome, more lovely reality to which it points. As a member of Christ's church you are part of His bride, joined to Him for all eternity. One day there will be no more sex. For anyone. But every Christian – now and forever – enjoys a deep, mystical union with Christ which is far, far, far better than any physical experience that belongs in this world. All of us – single and married – need to keep reminding ourselves of this great truth. As we have already mentioned, John Piper's book on marriage contains a useful chapter on singleness, but it is still written by someone happily married. We also commend Andrea Trevenna's excellent book *The Heart of Singleness* (Epson, U.K.: The Good Book Company, 2014).

Some will find themselves single after being married – perhaps widowed or newly divorced. That's tough. They have tasted of God's good gift and it can be harder for some to do without something they knew and treasured than to never have experienced it in the first place. If that is you, then God promises sufficient grace for all we need. The answer is not to compound the emptiness with illicit sexual intimacy. Rather, it is to cast ourselves on the God who helps and encourages us through every trial and loss.

Perhaps you are an older single? We want to encourage you: this subject is still critical for you as you live in the world; as you pray for the younger men and women in the congregation; as you teach and instruct them.

WHAT IF ... I STRUGGLE WITH SAME-SEX ATTRACTION?

Thankfully, Christians are better today at being honest about our struggles, and that includes the struggle of same-sex attraction. We are clearer that *to struggle* is not the same as *to sin* and the world's open acceptance of homosexuality has actually made it easier for Bible believing Christians to both talk about these matters and be helpful towards one another as we all fight sin of many kinds.

Of the recent books and resources published, the website *Living Out* (www.livingout.org) is an excellent first stop, run by a group of Christians who are same-sex attracted, but committed to living according to biblical principles. One of the contributors, Sam Allberry, has also written a superb little volume *Is God Anti-Gay?* (Epson, U.K.: The Good Book Company, 2013). A longer book that is worth searching out is Wesley Hill's *Washed and Waiting* (Grand Rapids, Michigan: Zondervan, 2010).

It is also worth mentioning here that these resources are good for those who minister to people with same-sex attraction or know family and church members who need help in this area. Written from a slightly different angle, Alex Tylee's *Walking with Gay Friends* (Nottingham, U.K.: Inter-Varsity Press, 2007) will also be a great help.

WHAT IF ... WE STRUGGLE IN BED?

You're not alone. Or even unusual. According to Britain's National Survey of Sexual Attitudes and

Lifestyle, 42 per cent of men and 51 per cent of women have experienced sexual difficulties in the last twelve months. That's an extraordinarily high proportion. Approximately 10 per cent of both men and women suffer from serious stress as a result. For Christians these problems can be compounded. We know that sex is important in God's economy, but – frankly – we are rather inhibited when it comes to talking about it. That makes admitting a problem and sorting it out rather difficult.

Struggles are of many kinds. For some couples it's mismatched sexual drive. For others it's issues in the past, perhaps abuse. Some Christians have physical difficulties, often to do with long-term illness. For others still the problems are circumstantial – sharing rooms with children, for example. Struggles are varied and not uncommon.

No, you are not alone. Or even unusual. The good news is that there is help. At present, there is not a huge amount of specifically Christian counselling, though much secular sexual counselling is good and helpful. There are, however, some good books worth searching out. Here are some we've found useful.

The most fun to read whilst remaining useful is probably *Sheet Music: Uncovering the Secrets of Sexual Intimacy in Marriage* by Kevin Leman (Carol Stream, Illinois: Tyndale House, 2003). This American book is forthright without being crass, although it is occasionally cringe-worthy! It is a Christian book, though not particularly biblical, full of good advice and chatty help.

A franker book, but significantly more theologically robust, is the Australian *The Best Sex for Life* by Patricia Weerakoon (Sydney Australia: Growing Faith Books, 2013). We like this resource a lot and stock and promote it on Proclamation Trust bookstalls. A word of caution: Patricia is at times *very* direct, but we believe that is increasingly (in our sex-saturated world) a useful and appropriate approach. As far as we know, this is one of the only Christian sex books which makes the clear points that we've been making in this book, about the link between sexual intimacy and the union Christ and the church share. Her theology is influenced by Christopher Ash, John Piper, Tim Keller and Andreas Köstenberger; it therefore has a strong foundation.

She has also written a book for teenagers on sex. Again, this is a frank read, but may be just what your children or kids in the church need to hear. It's called *Teen Sex by the Book* (Sydney, Australia: Youthworks, 2013). Our kids get lots of graphic input at school and a direct book which presents a biblical view may be the right way to tackle worldliness when it comes to sex.

A quite different kind of book is *Intimacy Ignited* by Joseph & Linda Dillow and Peter & Lorraine Pintus (Colorado Springs, CO: Navpress, 2004). This is two couples' reading of the Bible book of Song of Songs. You may not be persuaded by all their exegesis, but this book is designed to get a couple talking frankly, honestly and carefully about sex together.

Finally, Douglas Rosenau's *A Celebration of Sex* (Nashville, Tennessee: Thomas Nelson, 2002) is more of a classic 'how to' book on sex. Rosenau is a professor of human sexuality at the Psychological Studies Institute and is able to write carefully and appropriately about sex. It goes without saying that none of these books are ones to leave on the coffee table! However, they are all – to some extent – Christian books written for Christians.

WHAT IF ... WE'RE JUST ABOUT TO GET MARRIED? Honeymoon sex can be gloriously liberating or painfully disappointing. It may sound like a cliché, but sex is like playing the violin: it improves with practice. Therefore, it is important for couples to prepare for their honeymoon with the same carefulness that they plan their finances, for example. This book is not designed to be a manual for honeymooners, but there are resources that are written specifically for that task.

Don't let someone buy you one of the books above and leave you to get on with it. You will be overwhelmed. Rather, start slow! Greg and Amelia Clarke's short book (about the same length as this volume) is excellent. It is called *One Flesh: A Practical Guide to Honeymoon Sex and Beyond* (Kingsford, Australia: Matthias Press, 2001) and contains some helpful biblical and practical guidance. In addition, many marriage books or courses contain helpful sections. Brian & Barbara Edwards, *No Longer Two* (Leominster, U.K.: Day One, 2009) has a nicely old-fashioned, but nonetheless extremely helpful, section on sex for those preparing for marriage.

WHAT IF ... I'VE SINNED?

We are often tempted to think that we are the only people who struggle with sin. This is especially true when it comes to sexual sin as we know only too well that the church takes a rightly dim view of immorality. This guilt can leave us refusing to admit our problems and get the help we need, either from God or from the assistance He gives us through others in the congregation. Jesus says that sin, including sexual sin, begins in the heart. In fact:

> I tell you that anyone who looks at a woman lustfully has already committed adultery with her in his heart (Matt. 5:28).

On this basis, few come to their wedding night (for example) completely sin*less*. We need to recognise the sexual brokenness that many of us have deep in our hearts. Nevertheless, there *is* a difference between lustful thoughts that remain deep in our heart (which need to be confessed) and those that explode out into action. You may be a recently converted Christian and have a chequered sexual past. You may be a keen Christian, but you have a period in the past where you have backslidden and sinned. Or there may be a pattern of behaviour in your past that has affected your view of sex now. All this may be true and more besides.

We must be careful not to downplay sin. But neither must we ignore the full forgiveness offered to us in the gospel of Christ. His atoning death removes our sin from us and makes us new. It does not change or alter the past: we are what we are. Nevertheless, His Spirit convinces us that our sins are forgiven and gives us both the will and power to put sin to death. The power of cancelled sin is broken. John Piper has written a moving blog post about this topic called 'Walking the wedding aisle without your virginity.' You may find it helpful.[1]

Of course, once couples are married, sin can still arise. Singles too struggle in this area. The general principles still stand. In the gospel of Christ there is always both forgiveness and power to change. We need not be conformed to the world. But God wants us to be transformed and has committed Himself to that work in us.

WHAT IF ... I'M BATTLING WITH PORN?

This also is the advice we offer to those many Christians who have got themselves hooked on porn. All the evidence shows this is a common problem. We shouldn't be surprised at that given the ready availability and the world's acceptance of pornography as an acceptable means of stimulation for self-pleasure.

Pornography addiction is – at its root – a heart issue. Our sins come from our hearts and to stop sinning we need heart change. For many, that is easier said than done. Nevertheless, in this particular area there is lots of help. One of the

---

1.   It can be accessed at http://bit.ly/1rXXA2a

best resources is Tim Chester's excellent volume *Captured by a Better Vision* (Nottingham, U.K.: Inter-Varsity Press, 2010).[2]

There are also practical steps families can take to protect computers in the house. For many years we have used an internet filter such as Covenant Eyes or Safe Eyes. These also have features for Smart Phones. More recently we have activated filters installed by all U.K. broadband providers (a government requirement here in the U.K. since January 2014). These filters cover all devices in the house accessing the Internet via WiFi. Of course, it is possible to circumvent such filters and that is why addressing the issues of the heart is so key. But as with all sin there is both forgiveness and power to change.

WHAT IF ... I'VE BEEN ABUSED?

Sexual abuse is a painful and serious subject. We are grateful that the U.K. authorities are better at recognising and dealing with its effects, both by prosecuting perpetrators, but also by supporting those who have been abused. Sadly, as the press often gleefully reports, this is a problem both within the church as well as outside it. It is well known that sexual abuse in the past can also produce difficulties in current relationships and Christians are not immune from this historical effect.

Any brief advice offered in this area can seem remarkably trite and simplistic, especially to those who have suffered long-term abuse. However, there is help available – both secular and Christian, and we do

---

2. This is published in the U.S. under the title *Closing the window.*

urge you to seek it out. One book we have found of particular help is by Justin and Lindsey Holcomb. It is called *Rid of My Disgrace* (Wheaton, Illinois: Crossway, 2011) and – in our opinion – should be required reading for every minister and pastoral worker serving in twenty-first century Western society.

WHAT IF ... WE CAN'T HAVE SEX?

There are some couples for whom sex is impossible, sometimes painfully so. You may suffer with a particular debilitating illness that prevents intimacy. You may be apart for a length of time for any number of reasons. These may be short seasons, or longer periods. Perhaps the positive view of sex we've tried to convey has compounded the pain? We're sorry if that is the case; we certainly have no intention to wound.

What we all need to learn is that sexual intimacy is an expression of the marriage covenant, but it is not the covenant itself. In other words, though sex should be a normal part of marriage (1 Cor. 7), it cannot always be. We should not voluntarily give it up. But circumstances may prevent the intimacy that other couples enjoy. If God sovereignly sends these circumstances, we have to accept His wisdom and rejoice that what we do have, still points us towards the ultimate reality – Christ and His church.

AND WHAT IF ... ?

There are plenty more issues that you may need to deal with. We can't possibly list them all. However, two sets of similar resources are worth searching out. DayOne, a U.K. publisher, produce a set of short booklets called *'Help!'* addressing specific issues like, for example, *'Help! My Marriage has Grown Cold.'* A list is included on their website.[3] The Christian Counselling and Education Foundation (CCEF) produce a similar set of mini books, but with a more extensive range. Many of these deal directly with sexual issues.[4]

---

3.   http://www.dayone.co.uk/collections/books/help

4.   http://www.ccef.org/resources/minibooks

6

A CLOSING WORD

One of the seven angels who had the seven
bowls full of the seven last plagues came and
said to me, 'Come, I will show you the bride,
the wife of the Lamb.' And he carried me away
in the Spirit to a mountain great and high, and
showed me the Holy City, Jerusalem, coming
down out of heaven from God. It shone with
the glory of God, and its brilliance was like
that of a very precious jewel, like a jasper, clear
as crystal.

Rev. 21:9-11

We recently visited a small, provincial museum
in northern France, dedicated to the work of
the painter Henri Matisse (1869-1954). The museum was located in the town where he was born,
Le Cateau-Cambrésis. The museum had managed
to acquire a good number of his paintings and
sculptures – unusual for a small town exhibition. It
was a particularly enjoyable trip, enhanced by the
audio guide, narrated in heavily-accented English.
The narrator encouraged us to remember just one

painting, to focus on it and remember its detail and colour so that we would take something away in our memory.

The same approach is one we'd encourage with this book. Only, in this case, we want to tell you which painting we want you to remember. It's the picture that God has given us in marriage, and in particular in sexual intimacy. Marriage is the portrait of Christ and the union He enjoys with His church, the Bride for whom He died. Sex is the ultimate and joyful expression of that union.

So, enjoy sex, understand sex, treasure sex, delight in sex. And as you do so, remember the greater truth to which it points. Sexual fulfilment is a temporary reality. It lasts only for as long as couples are married, and even then can wax and wane according to the seasons of life. Even in a healthy, active marriage, sex is not everything – nor should it be.

Nevertheless, those brief moments of indescribable ecstasy which couples enjoy are a deep and momentous reminder – an enacted parable, as one writer puts it – of an eternal, everlasting, every-moment truth. Christ has died for His Bride, His church and will one day present her to Himself as a 'radiant church, without stain or wrinkle or any other blemish, but holy and blameless' (Eph. 5:27). This is our glorious future and God has been gracious enough to give us a sign of it now. Perhaps, then, we should leave the closing words to the Spirit-inspired Bible writers.

Husbands,

> May your fountains be blessed, and may you rejoice in the wife of your youth. A loving doe, a graceful deer – may her breasts satisfy you always, may you ever be intoxicated with her love (Prov. 5:18-19).

And wives, may you always be singing,

> Awake, north wind, and come, south wind!
> Blow on my garden, that its fragrance may spread everywhere.
> Let my beloved come into his garden and taste its choice fruits (Songs 4:16).

FURTHER READING

In addition to the books listed above, you may find some of the following resources useful.

Ash, C., *Marriage: Sex in the Service of God* (Nottingham: IVP Books, 2003)

Christopher's longer book on marriage is a thoughtful and carefully argued analysis of marriage in God's purposes. It strongly asserts the purpose of marriage (and sex within that) as a means to serve God in partnership. Christopher interacts with many other writers, including Barth's influential writing on marriage. This book is aimed at the pastor or scholar and will reward some time investment.

Burk, D., *What is the the Meaning of Sex?* (Wheaton, Illinois: Crossway, 2013)

Denny's well-reviewed book is essentially aiming to do what we are doing here, but at a more detailed level. It is a thorough analysis which also interacts with some of the current issues, including homosexuality. A lot of technical information, for example interaction with Greek, is kept in the extensive footnotes, so it is accessible for the 'ordinary' Christian.

Piper, J. and Taylor, J. (eds), *Sex and the Supremacy of Christ* (Wheaton, Illinois: Crossway, 2005)
This collection of essays is taken from the Desiring God National Conference in 2004. Contributors include the editors, Al Mohler, Mark Dever and C.J. Mahaney. As with any multi-author volume the contributions are somewhat mixed in their usefulness, but both of us enjoyed reading this book and it gave us a lot of food for thought. There are some particularly useful historical insights regarding both Luther and the Puritans, the latter sometimes getting a rather unfounded reputation for being anti-sex.

MARRIAGE BOOKS
There seem to be more books on marriage than almost any other genre. You will find books in your local Christian bookstore by Christopher Ash, John Piper, Tim & Kathy Keller, Mark & Grace Driscoll, John & Ann Benton, Paul Tripp, Alistair Begg – to name just a few! Everybody seems to have their favourites, but for our money we think Christopher's shorter book and John Piper's are the most theologically robust and pastorally useful.

Ash, C., *Married for God* (Nottingham: IVP Books, 2007)

Piper, J., *This Momentary Marriage* (Nottingham, IVP Books, 2009)

Christian Focus Publications

Our mission statement –

STAYING FAITHFUL

In dependence upon God we seek to impact the world through literature faithful to His infallible Word, the Bible. Our aim is to ensure that the Lord Jesus Christ is presented as the only hope to obtain forgiveness of sin, live a useful life and look forward to heaven with Him.

Our Books are published in four imprints:

CHRISTIAN
FOCUS

popular works including biographies, commentaries, basic doctrine and Christian living.

CHRISTIAN
HERITAGE

books representing some of the best material from the rich heritage of the church.

MENTOR

books written at a level suitable for Bible College and seminary students, pastors, and other serious readers. The imprint includes commentaries, doctrinal studies, examination of current issues and church history.

CF4•K

children's books for quality Bible teaching and for all age groups: Sunday school curriculum, puzzle and activity books; personal and family devotional titles, biographies and inspirational stories – Because you are never too young to know Jesus!

Christian Focus Publications Ltd,
Geanies House, Fearn, Ross-shire,
IV20 1TW, Scotland, United Kingdom
www.christianfocus.com